THE LAST YEARS OF STEAM
—AROUND—
CENTRAL WALES

THE LAST YEARS OF STEAM

—AROUND—

CENTRAL WALES

MICHAEL CLEMENS

FONTHILL

Above: The view from Builth Road (High Level) looking north up the old Mid-Wales Railway in 1958.

Page 1: By the summer of 1964, steam-hauled passenger trains were becoming a rarity at Carmarthen. No. 7827 *Lydham Manor* stands ready with the 5.50 p.m. to Aberystwyth.

Page 2: Great Western branch line delight, as No. 7437 prepares to leave Aberayron for Lampeter on 3 September 1964.

Fonthill Media Language Policy

Fonthill Media publishes in the international English language market. One language edition is published worldwide. As there are minor differences in spelling and presentation, especially with regard to American English and British English, a policy is necessary to define which form of English to use. The Fonthill Policy is to use the form of English native to the author.

Fonthill Media Limited
Fonthill Media LLC
www.fonthillmedia.com
office@fonthillmedia.com

First published in the United Kingdom
and the United States of America 2015

British Library Cataloguing in Publication Data:
A catalogue record for this book is available from the British Library

Typeset in 10.5pt on 13pt Sabon Lt Std
Printed and bound in England
Connect with us
 facebook.com/fonthillmedia twitter.com/fonthillmedia

Introduction

The most significant feature of this book compared to others about the railways of Central Wales in the days of steam is the photography. While little of the written detail will probably be new, virtually all of the photographs—a glorious combination of colour and black and white—have never been published before. This is my seventh railway photo-book, and it is made up almost entirely from photographs taken by my late father and me plus two of his pals. The period covered is approximately the ten years or so from the mid–1950s until 1966, and it will appeal to enthusiasts, modellers, and those with an interest in local history.

No. 1420 shunts in the goods shed at Kington in September 1964, just days before closure. There were special instructions issued for this because of the restricted clearance.

My father, C. N. 'Jim' Clemens (1922–1987), set out to record the railways of Britain and the steam locomotives that worked over them when the network was still largely intact. But what I don't think my father realised at the time is the tremendous interest there is nowadays in old railways and nostalgia generally, fifty or so years after the photographs were taken. On his visits to Central Wales he would often be accompanied by some of his chums, and as long as it was not during term-time at school, I would also generally be there. Although most of these old friends are now dead, I have been very fortunate in being allowed to use the material of some in this book. You will see the names of Dennis Bath (1925–2008) and Alan Maund (1930–1983) mentioned in various photographic credits; their excellent material was included thanks to the permission of their widows. Eric Parker (1900–1988) was a great stickler for the written record, and his diaries have been a priceless source of information in compiling many of the commentaries.

The delightful Welshpool & Llanfair Light Railway is featured under BR ownership in the 1950s, and also as here, in the early days of preservation. (*Alan Maund's collection*)

In broad terms, the area covered in this book is that to the south of the railway from Shrewsbury to Aberystwyth, to the west of the Welsh Marches Line from Shrewsbury to Abergavenny, and to the north of the A40 road from Abergavenny to Carmarthen. More specifically, it begins at Brecon, which for nearly 100 years prior to 1962 had been the starting point of four separate rural routes—all of these saw their passenger services withdrawn by the end of December that year. Less than 4 miles east of Brecon was Talyllyn Junction, and here was reputed to be the oldest railway tunnel still in use in the whole of the British Isles at the time. Talyllyn was also seen as an example of the GWR's inheritance of Welsh railway junctions in unlikely and/or inconvenient locations. The curiously named Three Cocks Junction was about 12 miles from Brecon, and here the Mid-Wales and Hereford, Hay & Brecon Railways converged, the station's name deriving from a medieval coaching inn.

The railway from Brecon to Three Cocks Junction skirted Llangorse Lake; here it is in the snowy weather of December 1962.

Hay-on-Wye shared a peculiar characteristic with another station we will visit later in this book, in that the station was in one country (England), but the town was in another (Wales). Judging by the date of these Hay-on-Wye photographs (1958), my father was using a German Super Baldina 35-mm camera coupled with Ilford FP3 film, and the results look superb. Those from earlier years are sadly not as good, and the only examples of these are on a favourite line of my father's—The Golden Valley Railway from Hay-on-Wye to Pontrilas. This line is featured in a montage of photographs taken between 1948 and 1954, the oldest of which are only the size of a thumbnail. But at the junction station of Pontrilas in 1962 is an example of arguably the best (but expensive) colour film of its day, Kodachrome II, with its superb colour rendition. Returning to Hay-on-Wye, we continue our journey along the River Wye to Hereford visiting Eardisley, Almeley, Kinnersley, and Moorhampton on the way.

Leominster was a railway crossroads on the main line from Shrewsbury to Hereford that runs from north to south, and is today called the Marches Line. Coming in from the east was the line from Bromyard: this had closed in 1952, but the track had been left in position, thus allowing a very final departure from

This 1965 view at the east end of Machynlleth Station includes the newly built goods shed on the right; the original is featured in the body of this book. (*Alan Maund's collection*)

Craven Arms to Llanelly was 90 miles, but the route via Cardiff and Newport was over 50 per cent longer, and in 1960 considerable freight traffic was forecast to pass over this hilly and rural line, but it came to nothing. Local passenger traffic was sparse, and in 1962 it was revealed that in the 60 miles between Llandovery and Craven Arms only two intermediate stations were taking more than £5 per day in receipts (Llandrindod Wells and Knighton). This line endured numerous closure proposals, but, unlike many other country routes in Britain, it surprisingly survived them all and is still open today.

Probably the most famous, but certainly not the highest, summit on the old Cambrian Railways system was that at Talerddig on the main line from Newtown, Moat Lane Junction, and Carno to Machynlleth. It gave the opportunity for enthusiasts to witness steam locomotives working hard on their way to and from the coast, especially on summer Saturdays when extra services were arranged to carry the holidaymakers; my 12th birthday in 1963 was spent here watching all the activity. Also near the summit was, at the time of its construction, the deepest railway cutting in the world. This was a huge engineering achievement of its era and we see a *Manor* blasting its way uphill through it. Descending to the coast

Reputed to be the oldest railway tunnel still in use in the British Isles at the time—Talyllyn Tunnel as viewed from the junction station in 1958.

No. 80098 fills its tanks at the old Welshpool Station on 14 January 1965. Today, this trackbed forms part of the A483 Welshpool by-pass.

we pass by Commins Coch and Cemmes Road on our way to Machynlleth, then as now a hub of the local railway system. The station area is covered extensively, including the locomotive depot and the old Corris Railway station, before arrival at probably the most famous of all the Welsh remote junctions—Dovey Junction, a station with no road access.

After Borth time is spent at Aberystwyth looking at the standard-gauge station and engine shed, before a visit to Aberystwyth's cliff railway and a trip on the Vale of Rheidol Railway to Aberffrwd and Devil's Bridge. The legendary Manchester & Milford Railway never reached either of the places mentioned in its title, but instead ended up as a 40-mile-long railway running south from Aberystwyth. Onwards through Caradog Falls Halt, Strata Florida, and Tregaron to Lampeter, a junction for something of a latecomer to the railway map—the by-this-time freight-only branch line through Felin Fach to Aberayron. This delightful country terminus is visited in September 1964, with your author being privileged to ride back to Lampeter in the cab of pannier tank No. 7437. Pencader was the terminus of the M&MR and also junction for the branch to Newcastle Emlyn via Llandyssul and Henllan. This was another branch the author's party travelled along on the daily freight train in September 1964. At last, we reach journey's end at Carmarthen via Llanpumpsaint and Conwil.

When these photographs were taken, both my father and I were largely ignorant of Welsh pronunciations and spellings. It was many decades before I

The Mid-Wales Railway followed the River Wye for about 30 miles; a Brecon to Moat Lane-Junction train gets close to the river in December 1962.

was instructed in pronunciation by my friend and author of Welsh railway books Gwyn Briwnant-Jones. And while I am much better now (but still learning), I am still left with the problem of spellings. This is a most difficult area, with both the railway companies and the places concerned changing their spellings over the years. For instance, the signs at the railway station in 1964 might have said 'Aberayron', but today it is spelt 'Aberaeron'. A nearby station with three different spellings was variously 'Llandyssil', 'Llandyssul', and 'Llandysul'. I apologise in advance for any mistakes of this nature that I am sure will have been made.

Finally, I would like to thank various societies and individuals who have freely given me their help in the making of this book: David Postle of the Kidderminster Railway Museum for providing me with some of the Central Wales Line photographs from the museum's archive, and also his efforts (including contacting R. A. Cooke) in finding detail about Titley Junction; David Evans (Jr), who trawled through his late father David Evans (Sr)'s photographic archive to precisely identify the date of the last train to Presteign; the Monmouthshire Railway Society, particularly their chairman John Livsey; the Severn Valley Railway Association (Stourbridge Branch); the Shirley Railway Club, and the Tewkesbury YMCA Railway Club.

Michael Clemens,
Pershore, Worcestershire.
December 2014.

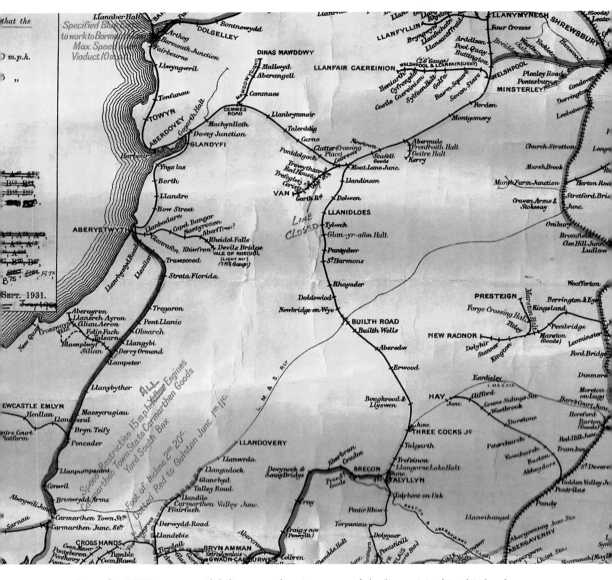

Part of a GWR route availability map showing most of the lines visited in this book.

TALYLLYN TUNNEL
674 YARDS
OPENED BY THE HAY RAILWAY
7 MAY 1816
JOHN HODGKINSON ENGINEER
ENLARGED AND RE-OPENED BY THE
BRECON AND MERTHYR RAILWAY
1 MAY 1863
HENRY CONYBEARE ENGINEER
THIS PLAQUE WAS SET UP BY THE BRECON CHAMBER OF TRADE
IN THE YEAR OF THE FESTIVAL OF BRITAIN — 1951

Two more photographs at Talyllyn Junction, but this time at the east end of the station. The colour (Ektachrome) view dates from 13 December 1962 and shows No. 46511 ready to depart on the right-hand track with the lunchtime through-service from Brecon to Moat Lane Junction, a distance of just under 60 miles. These Ivatt Class 2 2-6-0s were specially constructed at Swindon in the early 1950s for use on this route, replacing the Victorian-built Dean Goods 0-6-0s. On the opposite platform is the rear coach of the pannier tank-hauled 11.15 a.m. Newport-to-Brecon service; this has entered the station on the far left-hand track and will soon be passing through Talyllyn Tunnel. The timetable was well thought-out here and good connections were the norm. In the foreground is the Cambrian Railways-built extension platform, this was added in the 1890s on the upside of the north curve and allowed long trains from Brecon to clear the single-track through the tunnel at the other end of the station. The signal box is Talyllyn West Junction, and by the summer of 1959 it opened at 6.30 a.m. and closed at 10.15 p.m.—except on Saturdays when it closed at 10.45 p.m. (it did not open on Sundays). The finger boards showing various destinations, around 1960, were adjacent to the signal box so as to be in front of passengers as they walked over the barrow crossing, there being no footbridge here.

In the previous photograph at Talyllyn Junction Station itself, we could see the two diverging routes—the B&M heading south, and the MWR going north. There was also a direct link between these two routes avoiding Talyllyn Junction Station itself that created a triangle of lines, this allowing a direct service between South and North Wales. This view is taken from a Three Cocks Junction–bound train on 30 October 1958 at Talyllyn North Junction. On the right can just be made out the double-track from Talyllyn Junction Station, which converged to single at the north junction. The buildings visible are of the former typically wooden MWR station which originally had platforms on both sides—the left to Merthyr and the right to Brecon—and had closed in 1878. This east loop consisted of a single through-running line, alongside which was both an inner and outer siding. By the date of this photograph, the through passenger trains between Cardiff and Aberystwyth that once passed over the east loop were no more than a distant memory. But the famous ammonia tanks freight train between Tees-side and Dowlais, which started coming this way from 1955 onwards (after re-routing away from the Abergavenny–Merthyr line), used the east loop until 1962.

At Three Cocks Junction, the lines from Hereford (on the right) and Builth Wells (on the left) joined together for the onward journey to Brecon, the different 'change for' destinations on the respective station nameboards. All three photographs were taken on the same Sunday in the summer of 1958. The Hereford line was constructed by the HH&BR, whereas that coming from the north and onwards to Talyllyn Junction was built by the MWR. The station buildings and signal box were built on a triangular platform between the two routes. Both lines had passing loops and there were sidings at the Brecon end of the station. The station was built by the MWR, and the boundary with the HH&BR was 29 chains towards Hereford. The MWR had planned a north-to-east curve allowing a direct route from Builth Wells to Hereford, but this was never built. All the lines radiating from Three Cocks Junction were single-track, but a long-standing disagreement obstructed plans for doubling the track onwards to Talyllyn Junction. By the early 1900s, the protagonists were now the Cambrian and the Midland Railways, successors to the MWR and HH&BR. The MR was not in favour of double-track and it went to arbitration in 1909, the judgement going against the CR. The tickets are dated 5 January 1961.

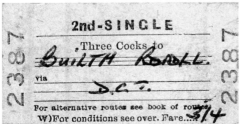

These two photographs at Hay-on-Wye were taken in the summer of 1958. The station was originally simply known as 'Hay', but in 1947 the town's name was changed to 'Hay-on-Wye' by the Urban District Council, the station's name following suit in June 1955. The first photograph shows the view a little to the west of the station above Bailey Walk and the banks of the River Wye, the nearest signal being an LMS-type upper quadrant. This reflects the line's history as it was the route the MR used to reach its network of lines around Swansea. In 1903 the line through Hay was continuously open, day and night, except between 6.00 a.m. and midnight on Sundays. Barely visible just before the station is the bridge over Dulas Brook and this marked the boundary between Wales and England, the station in England and the town in Wales. At the station itself the main buildings were on the down platform, with just the signal box and a small waiting room on the up. By the summer of 1959, there were four weekday passenger services each way plus a morning school train, but loadings were light. Local freight traffic was also light, the ammonia trains being the only reminder of the former through-traffic. All this came to an end on and from 31 December 1962, although Hay-on-Wye goods shed facilities were retained as a non-rail-connected depot with a BR lorry available to fetch and carry to a railhead.

In a very rural corner of Herefordshire was a railway that became a by-word for an economic lost cause—the Golden Valley Railway from Hay to Pontrilas. It initially garnered much local enthusiasm, despite some warning signs. The first stage from Pontrilas to Dorstone was authorised in 1876 and the extension on to Hay the year after; the first part opened in 1881, followed by the complete line by 1889. Nine years later it was all closed down.

As with many rural lines, Hay to Pontrilas conjured visions of greater things to come and the chairman of the company, Sir Richard Green-Price MP for Radnor, had thoughts of a link to Monmouth and even Bristol. Investments in the line and its extensions totalled about £335,000, but when it was eventually sold to the GWR in 1899, it was for a mere £9,000—quite a financial disaster.

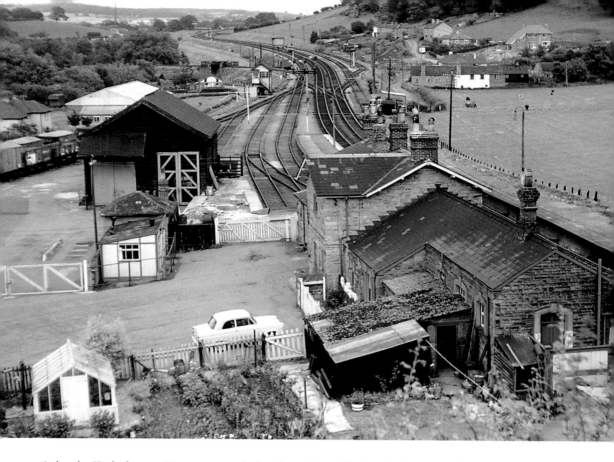

A lovely Kodachrome II panorama dating from June 1962 and facing north from above Pontrilas Station. The main line is that from Hereford to Abergavenny, the station here losing its passenger service on 9 June 1958, as did other local stations along the route. The bay platform and run-round loop for the Golden Valley branch can be seen, plus there are some wagons in the goods yard. The bridge over the A465 is visible in the distance and still gave rail access (until 1969) to the Elm Bridge Ordinance Depot on the sole remaining part of the Golden Valley branch. This bridge was removed during road widening and just the abutments on the east side remain today. The Golden Valley branch locomotive was kept in an engine shed at Pontrilas, but this was out of sight, a little way up the branch itself. In 1949, the only time that the Pontrilas signal box was not open was between 8.00 p.m. on Sundays and 1.15 a.m. on Mondays. Also visible in the distance are the up and down running loops, both of sixty-five-wagon capacity.

Opposite and pages 24-25: The GWR reopened the line in 1901 and generated a healthy return on their investment. But decline set in again after the development of road transport following the First World War. The Second World War saw the expansion of freight traffic, and in particular an ammunition depot was built between Pontrilas and Abbeydore, but the passenger service ceased in 1941. The last through-train to Hay ran on 31 December 1949, and beyond Abbeydore the service closed at the end of January 1953. The photographs all date from between 1948 and 1954 and start at the top with Green's Siding, where this platform and shelter were a later opening by the GWR. Next seen is the goods yard on the other side of the B4352 road bridge at Green's Siding. Then comes Dorstone, followed by Peterchurch, Bacton (another halt opened by the GWR), and Abbeydore.

One of your author's earliest railway memories is of this special train, the Stephenson Locomotive Society's (SLS) last train from Abergavenny to Merthyr on 5 January 1958. This is the tour train at Abergavenny (Monmouth Road) behind 0-8-0 No. 49121, where it is awaiting enthusiasts arriving on a service train from Birmingham. It went to Abergavenny Junction, where it joined forces with the now preserved LNWR 'Coal Tank' No. 58926 to do battle with the fearsome gradients on the line to Merthyr. It has already been mentioned in this book in connection with the four routes to Brecon, of which the first to open was the B&M, this also involving miles of formidable 1 in 38 gradients. One railway that was never built, despite it appearing in many ways to be an obvious candidate, was from Abergavenny to Brecon. This would have been a relatively straight-forward water-level route, with no steep gradients following the River Usk/Monmouthshire & Brecon Canal. It nearly came to fruition with the proposed Vale of Crickhowell Railway in the mid–1860s.

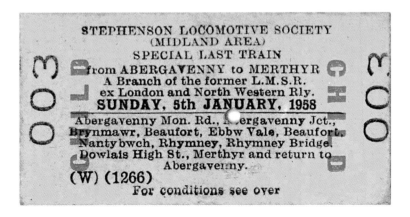

STEPHENSON LOCOMOTIVE SOCIETY
(MIDLAND AREA)
SPECIAL LAST TRAIN
from ABERGAVENNY to MERTHYR
A Branch of the former L.M.S.R.
ex London and North Western Rly.
SUNDAY, 5th JANUARY, 1958
Abergavenny Mon. Rd., Abergavenny Jct.,
Brynmawr, Beaufort, Ebbw Vale, Beaufort,
Nantybwch, Rhymney, Rhymney Bridge,
Dowlais High St., Merthyr and return to
Abergavenny.
(W) (1266)
For conditions see over

Returning to Hay-on-Wye and continuing our journey eastwards towards Hereford, this is the junction station of Eardisley. The railway we have followed from Brecon closely tracks that of the earlier horse-drawn tramway—the Hay Railway. This tramway had opened to Hay on 14 May 1816 and the extension on to Eardisley became operational on 1 December 1818. At Eardisley connection was to be made with another tramway—The Kington Railway—the Act for which received Royal Assent on 23 May 1818, and this opened on 7 August 1820. The Hay Railway Act of 1860 had enabled the later railway companies to use parts of the tramway for their respective lines, and now history repeated itself. The Kington & Eardisley Railway Act of 1862 authorised it to purchase the existing Kington Railway and to use such parts of this tramway as were required to make their new railway. In this view turned towards Hereford, taken from the A4111 road bridge in July 1959, the KER is seen branching off to the left. By this time, all that was left of the old KER was the short spur to a timber yard as pictured here (speed not to exceed 5 mph), and this had been lifted by January 1961. The ticket is undated.

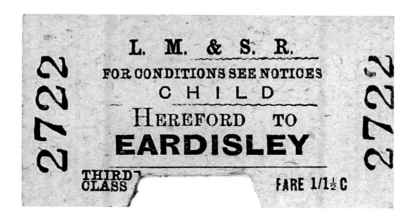

L. M. & S. R.
FOR CONDITIONS SEE NOTICES
CHILD
HEREFORD TO
EARDISLEY
THIRD CLASS   FARE 1/1½C
2722   2722

Taken on the same Sunday in July 1959 as the previous photograph at Eardisley, we are now at Almeley on the Kington & Eardisley Railway. The line through Almeley was opened on 3 August 1874 and worked by the GWR, which then purchased the local company outright on 1 July 1897. The line was steeply graded and climbed about 300 feet in about 3 miles at a gradient of 1 in 44 to 1 in 47 from the Eardisley end, Almeley station being inconveniently situated in the middle of the grade. Traffic was always light and the line was closed entirely on 1 January 1917, the track being taken up to be used in the war effort. It was re-laid and then re-opened from Titley Junction to Almeley on 18 September 1922, with the full service to Eardisley restored on 11 December 1922. The branch was closed again on 1 July 1940 and this time was not re-opened after the war. In 1964, my father was told by train crew at Kington that when the track through Almeley was finally taken up, a GWR 2251 Class 0-6-0 tender engine was used on the dismantling trains because of water capacity problems with the usual tank engines. The station building still exists today.

One mile and 60 chains further on from Eardisley Junction was Kinnersley. This is the view facing towards Hereford on a wet Sunday 13 March 1960, taken from the road bridge. The LMS triangular-shaped running-in board is prominent on the platform and allowed passengers to better sight it from the train. Another station sign is almost hidden by undergrowth at the far end of the station. There doesn't seem to be any freight traffic; nevertheless, the daily (except Sundays) freight train in the summer of 1954 called at 12.40 p.m. for ten minutes on its way from Hereford, and at 2.50 p.m. for fourteen minutes on its return, having started from Brecon at 8.20 a.m. When the passenger service was withdrawn at the end of 1962, a freight-only service was maintained from Hereford to Eardisley. However, freight facilities had been withdrawn at Kinnersley at the same time as the passenger service, so although these goods trains continued passing through, they did not call for custom, and even this came to an end in September 1964.

Moorhampton was the next station east towards Hereford. As at Kinnersley, this was taken on a wet day, but this time in February 1960. We are again looking east and from the road bridge over the station, but unlike Kinnersley, Moorhampton was provided with a passing loop. Visible on the platform are the weighing scales and behind them an oil lamp on the wooden station building, further along by the running-in board the lighting is on a post, plus there is also a vertical-type parcels trolley and an MR-style bench. The signal box was open from 7.35 a.m. until 8.50 p.m. (9.45 p.m. on Saturdays), but not at all on Sundays. The maximum speed allowed anywhere between Hereford and Three Cocks Junction was 45 mph, and all trains were subject to a 15 mph restriction on entering and leaving both the up and down loops here. Because there was only the one platform at Moorhampton, two passenger trains were not allowed to pass—only two freights or a passenger plus freight. As at Kinnersley, all services ceased at the end of December 1962, so the freight train to Eardisley which survived until September 1964 did not call here either.

Originally, trains bound for Brecon from Hereford used the Barton and Moorfields stations, but it was the station here at Barrs Court which was used from 1893 onwards (the station is still open today). Barrs Court had been built following an 1854 agreement between the Shrewsbury & Hereford Railway and the Hereford, Ross & Gloucester Railway; it originally had both standard and broad gauges. When the Midland Railway started their Brecon services from here they employed their own booking clerks, and a bay platform was provided at the northern end of Barrs Court for these trains. However, on 11 October 1962 (the date of the ticket), No. 46503 is leaving Hereford from the adjacent through-platform with the lunchtime service that ran only to Three Cocks Junction, linking up there with a train that came down the MWR to provide an onward connection to Brecon. Departures towards Brecon from Barrs Court were quite complex and involved a reversal of direction, plus the negotiation of various junctions. After travelling in a northerly direction for about 30 chains, No. 46503 will arrive at the Brecon Curve Junction signal box, and seen in the black & white photograph taken later that same day. In 1959 this signal box was open continuously and controlled the Brecon Curve that branches off to the left. By the time No. 46503 had negotiated this curve it would be facing south; more junctions and pointwork would then follow, before it reached the relative tranquillity of the single-track onwards to Three Cocks Junction.

The A44 road bridge at Leominster is host to a Gloucestershire-registered A35 van full of wood. Underneath it, however, there is plenty of railway interest in these photographs both taken on the same day in September 1964. The main line through Leominster, the nearest of the two tracks in the first view, was the Shrewsbury & Hereford Railway which opened in 1853. Shunting beyond in the west-side yards is No. 1420, preparing that day's freight train for the Kington and Presteign branches—it was allocated to the Hereford shed specifically for this kind of work. Heading north in the second photograph, with what appears to be a train of coke wagons, is Birkenhead-allocated LMS Crab No. 42827. No. 1420 has only 800-gallon-capacity water tanks and will top them up at the water column in front of No. 42827; it won't be able to take on any more water until Kington, over an hour and a half later. Nearest to the camera there has been some removal of track, and it was along here that the branch to Bromyard once ran. Today, the road layout at Leominster has been altered, and this bridge is used only by pedestrians and cyclists, while a new road bridge was built to the south; it connects with the new by-pass, part of which uses the track bed of the old Bromyard branch.

It is Sunday 26 April 1958, and this is the scene looking south from Leominster Station on the day of the last train over the branch to Bromyard. Normal service trains had worked for the last time over this route on Saturday 13 September 1952, but the track had been left in place until 1958. What would today's health and safety conscious world think of the mass of enthusiasts clambering all over the track? The SLS special was worked by 45xx 2-6-2T No. 4571, hauling six coaches, and departure back to Worcester was scheduled for 5.30 p.m. No. 4571 was a Worcester locomotive at this time, but would re-allocate all the way to Plymouth and then Penzance in 1959. In the distance pulling away on a passenger train to Hereford is No. 73133, one of the BR Standard Class 5s fitted with British-Caprotti valve gear. The bridge that the previous two photographs were taken from can just be made out too.

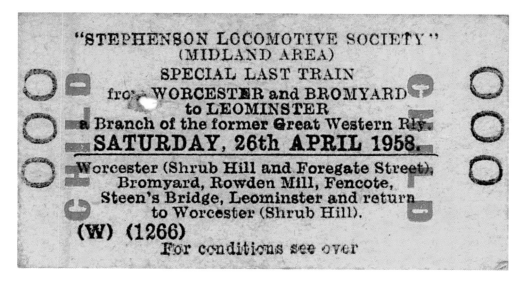

"STEPHENSON LOCOMOTIVE SOCIETY"
(MIDLAND AREA)
SPECIAL LAST TRAIN
from WORCESTER and BROMYARD
to LEOMINSTER
a Branch of the former Great Western Rly.
SATURDAY, 26th APRIL 1958.
Worcester (Shrub Hill and Foregate Street),
Bromyard, Rowden Mill, Fencote,
Steen's Bridge, Leominster and return
to Worcester (Shrub Hill).
(W) (1266)
For conditions see over

CHILD

CHILD

Departures for the Kington branch from Leominster headed northwards, 34 chains up the Shrewsbury & Hereford Railway to Kington Junction (pictured here), where they branched off to the west. In addition to controlling the railway junction, at the time of this photograph, the signal box also controlled the level crossing of the main A49 north–south road, and so was open continuously. Not so for the boxes at Leominster Station and Leominster South, which did shut at times during the night according to the summer 1959 working timetable. This view of the Kington Junction signal box dates from September 1964; its function, to control the Kington branch, would soon be no more, as the branch closed that month. The style of the signal box follows that of others along the main line, such as Leominster South and Marsh Brook (a listed building). Kington Junction signal box no longer exists today; there is still a busy level crossing here, but now of the automatic half-barrier type.

Opposite, above: The author's father visited the Kington and Presteign branches twice in 1964, and on 28 April was lucky enough to have permission to travel in the guard's van on the freight train. The weather that day was typical of the time of year—blustery and cold, with April showers interspersed with sunshine. Departure from Leominster was scheduled for 8.40 a.m. according to the permit, but it was 9.30 a.m. before the train got away with its load of three wagons. Eric Parker's diary says the fire in the brake van was much appreciated. This is Pembridge, and while there was some shunting to be done by No. 1420 at the previous station of Kingsland, there was no such business here. In the days of passenger trains, staff would open and shut the various crossing gates along the line; but by the time this was taken, the train crew already largely did it themselves, with the fireman generally opening the gates and the guard closing them. When the line was inspected on 22 July 1857 by the Board of Trade, a problem was discovered at Pembridge. An over bridge had been authorised in the Act of Parliament, but a level crossing had been constructed instead. It was agreed that the line could open but the company had to promise to obtain a second Act to legalise the crossing.

The 'level crossing' Act duly received its Royal Assent on 19 April 1859. The 1959 working timetable shows the single freight train (covering both branches) running daily except Sundays, but Parker's diary states that, by this time, it ran only on Tuesdays, Thursdays, and Saturdays (Kington only).

BRITISH TRANSPORT COMMISSION

NOT TRANSFERABLE.

FORM OF PERMIT FOR TRAVEL IN GUARD'S VAN
OR OTHER NON-PASSENGER CARRYING VEHICLE.

The bearer.................MR. C.N. CLEMENS.......................... is
authorised on payment of the appropriate fare to travel on the
................8.40 a.m................... freight train between
.........LEOMINSTER.............. and...KINGTON AND PRESTEIGN & Return
in the guard's van or other vehicle not usually provided for
the accommodation of passengers upon and subject to the release
and indemnity signed by the bearer or his employer.

* Available until further notice during the period of xxxxxxxxxxxxxx.
* Available only for use on the ......Tues day of...28/4/..19 64.

37

Titley might seem an unlikely place for a railway junction, but four lines, and each from a different point of the compass, eventually converged on this remote location in Herefordshire. The first to arrive ran from east to west: the Leominster & Kington Railway was authorised on 10 July 1854, and opened through Titley to Kington on 27 July 1857. In 1862 the L&KR was leased to the GWR, and on 1 July 1898 it amalgamated with the GWR while the local company was dissolved. Next to arrive was the Kington & Eardisley Railway from the south in 1874, and this line was described in the commentary about Almeley Station (page 30). Although a very small company, the K&ER obtained seven Acts of Parliament over thirteen years, and this included powers to build a line northwards to Presteign, the county town of Radnorshire. Not surprisingly with all this parliamentary activity, the K&ER didn't have the funds to build the line to Presteign, and the proposal was instead taken up by the L&KR, their Presteign branch opening on 9 September 1875. At the time of these photographs (complete with a 'Keystone Cops'-type gangers' velocipede), September 1964, total closure was only days away.

The branches to Eardisley and Presteign were operated to and from Kington. Combined with the Leominster to Kington services, this resulted in a lot of trains passing through Titley (one of the original stations on the L&K). Although only a single-track remained at this time, Titley used to be a passing station on the four single-track converging routes, and it could get quite busy. Looking at the summer 1936 working timetable, seven services passed through it in less than ninety minutes during the morning. Titley therefore used to have a station master, who was also responsible for the tiny Forge Crossing Halt on the Presteign branch. The station name is clearly displayed as 'Titley Junction', yet despite much research the station always seems to have officially been just plain 'Titley'. This was not something unique to Titley: discrepancies in the rendering of station names in timetables and other publications, and even on different nameboards around the stations themselves, were quite common, and this was commented on in the November 1958 edition of *Railway Magazine*. Although the railway through Titley had been freight-only since 1955, the station had its freight facilities withdrawn on 6 July 1959. The substantial station buildings are seen in September 1964 and survive today.

The first of these photographs shows the very final in-bound freight service from Kington to Presteign in September 1964. No. 1420 is descending the 1 in 53 grade to cross the Hindwell Brook, and also the border between England (Herefordshire) and Wales (Radnorshire). It has about 1 mile left before arriving at Presteign. Your author has spent much time trying to precisely date this significant final occasion in the railway history of Presteign, and has been able to identify it as Thursday 24 September 1964 thanks to the photographic archive of the late David Evans (an old family friend). A guard's van was positioned at either end to cater for local staff plus the odd enthusiast wanting to travel on this final in-bound train. There were three wagons in between, of which the rear two will be left at Presteign, so clearly there must have been at least one more train to Presteign to clear out remaining wagons. The second view is of the 28 April 1964 arrival at Presteign, again with No. 1420. Three wagons of gas pipes have been brought to the town, and there seems to be evidence of identical workings in the past judging from the similar wagons already in the goods yard.

The very last in-bound working to Presteign has now arrived at the town's station on 24 September 1964. No. 1420 has already run around the train but has yet to begin shunting in the goods yard. Notable is the spelling on the station sign—'Presteign', not the usual 'Presteigne'. The railway used the version without the 'e' until April 1952, which is said to be more Welsh. There must have been some dispute over which spelling to use, as examination of the station sign will reveal that the 'e' at the end has at some point been removed. The arrival of the railway in Presteign had an immediate impact in the form of a 5-shillings-per-ton reduction in the price of coal, since the hilly turnpike road from Knighton could now be avoided. But the town did not develop as expected: an anticipated distillery did not mature, and the population fell from 1,910 in 1875 to 1,250 about eighty years later. In 1936, there were only three passenger train arrivals and departures daily (none on Sundays), and of these two were mixed trains (passenger and freight together); there was also one dedicated freight service, which ran only when required. The passenger service ceased on 5 February 1951 because of the national coal crisis, temporarily at first, but it was never restored and closure officially became permanent from 4 June 1951. In 1959, there was a single daily freight train, but by the end of services in September 1964, this appears to have run on just two days a week.

By the mid–1860s, the K&ER owned the remaining portion of the old horse-drawn Kington Railway which carried on west of Kington to lime works at Burlinjobb. Output was increasing and it was inconvenient to transfer the traffic to the standard-gauge at Kington. This influenced the decision to construct a full-size railway westwards from Kington to New Radnor, a section of the K&ER isolated from the rest of its system. It opened on 25 September 1875 and was worked by the GWR. This extension required a new station to be built at Kington, slightly to the north of the L&KR's old terminus. Both photographs date from 28 April 1964. On the right of the colour view is the new through-station on the by now closed line to New Radnor: it was built by the K&ER and became joint with the L&KR. No. 1420 is shunting in the yard and its load of gas pipes for Presteign can be seen towards the left. On the extreme left is the original passenger terminus of the L&KR. This whole area was used as a goods depot and included a substantial goods shed. The black and white photograph shows the original terminus in detail; this generously sized building was both a house and station office, which included the booking hall and public areas. Nothing remains of the 'new' station today, but the original L&KR building survives as a private residence.

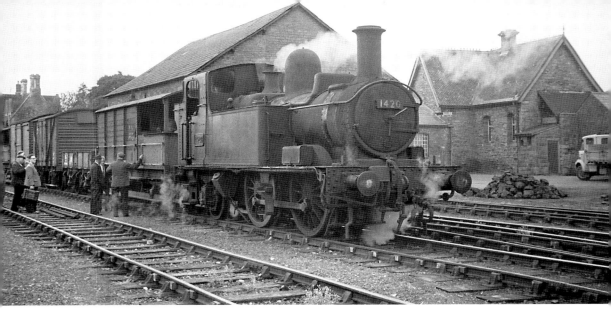

Two more photographs of the goods yard at Kington, but this time on 24 September 1964. No. 1420 is ready to work the very last in-bound freight service to Presteign. The old station building is in the background, and standing outside it is a rather puzzled-looking lady wearing an apron. The substantial goods shed can be studied in detail, the lean-to building in front seemingly used as a petrol store according to the sign on the door. There are plenty of railway staff present, no doubt wanting to make a final trip to Presteign and back. With the closure of both the Presteign and Kington branches that month, there was no more work for No. 1420. At the beginning of 1964 three of the class, all of which had received heavy repairs in 1961, were allocated to Hereford. No. 1447 was withdrawn in March, and No. 1458 was re-allocated to Gloucester in July to see out its time on the Chalford push-pull service, until this ceased in the November. This left just No. 1420 to soldier on alone in the final weeks at Hereford, until it too was re-allocated to Gloucester in October and withdrawn in November. However, No. 1420 survived to be preserved and was sold in running order to the Dart Valley Railway in Devon. It arrived there in October 1965, and is still with us today.

Above and opposite: Formal opening of the railway in to Kington from Leominster took place on 27 July 1857, and to celebrate this exactly 100 years later, the 'Kington Centenary' rail tour was organised by the SLS. The tour had started from Tenbury Wells, where connection was made with a normal service train for passengers from the Birmingham direction. Passenger services on the Leominster to New Radnor and Presteign sections were withdrawn, due to the coal crisis, on 5 February 1951. However, the service was restored solely between Leominster and Kington on 2 April 1951, and this carried on until 7 February 1955. Thus, at the time of this centenary tour no scheduled passenger trains were running through Kington, but freight was. The tour is seen at the 'new' Kington Station on 27 July 1957, on its way west to Dolyhir. It was not possible to travel beyond Dolyhir as the section on to New Radnor had its remaining freight service withdrawn on 31 December 1951. No. 1455 was scheduled to stop at Kington from 4.20 p.m. until 4.32 p.m., and judging from the wet platform behind the two men, it filled up its water tanks here, too. No. 1455 had been working locally since 1941 and was another of this class to make Gloucester its final home, working the Golden Valley service and being withdrawn in May 1964. (*Dennis Bath's collection*)

KINGTON

S·L·S SPECIAL

LEOMINSTER
KINGTON
CENTENARY

1455

2nd - SPECIAL ARRANGEMENT
STEPHENSON LOCOMOTIVE SOCIETY
(MIDLAND AREA)
KINGTON CENTENARY RAIL
TOUR
SATURDAY, 27th JULY 1957

036

036

Tenbury Wells, Woofferton, Leominster,
Kington, Dolyhir, Kington, Titley, Presteign,
Titley, Leominster and Woofferton.

(W) (1266)

For conditions see over

The lime kilns at Burlinjobb were the stated destination in the 1818 plans for the Kington Railway which started from Eardisley. They were one of its major sources of traffic. This traffic transferred from the tramway to the K&ER when it opened west of Kington in 1875. From late December 1951 onwards, the furthest west from Kington that trains could reach was here at Dolyhir, and this for freight only, the passenger service having ceased on 5 February 1951. This was supposedly a temporary closure, but a passenger service never did run again and it was officially made permanent as of 4 June 1951. No. 1455 is standing at Dolyhir Station on 27 July 1957, with the 'Kington Centenary' rail tour made up of a two-coach auto set and scheduled to arrive at 4.50 p.m. Dolyhir was once a prize-winner in the GWR's well-kept station garden competition. Despite quarrying still taking place at Dolyhir today, it would appear that little traffic came the way of the railway in later years, although in 1936 the down goods train was allowed 30 minutes to shunt here. In the September 1957 *Railway Magazine* it was stated that the section west of Kington was unlikely to remain in use for much longer—and so it proved, with complete closure occurring on 9 June 1958. (*Dennis Bath's collection*)

Opposite: Two more photographs on the occasion of the 'Kington Centenary' rail tour on 27 July 1957, and filmed from the B4355 road bridge just to the west of the 'new' station at Kington. Looking east, the railway bridge over the Gilwern Brook (or Back Brook) is prominent; both the tramway (Kington Railway) plus the later standard-gauge railway followed this watercourse. The original station (by now the goods depot and yard) is out of sight to the right of this picture, the large water tank feeding the water columns at Kington being visible on the left. Looking in the other direction, towards Dolyhir and New Radnor, is the engine shed. This had opened in 1875 and in later years had an allocation of two 58xx 0-4-2Ts; on 31 December 1947, these were Nos 5808 and 5814. It was a standard branch line shed with brick walls and a slate roof, measuring approximately 60 feet by 20 feet. There were three crews and they performed all the various branch workings except the weekday goods to and from Leominster. The shed closed on 5 February 1951. Once the railway was opened west of Kington, the tramway was closed too, and because much of its land was roadside verge it was sold or made over to the turnpike trustees. (*Dennis Bath's collection*)

Above: The furthest west that the railway reached from Kington was here at New Radnor, but all traffic had ceased by the end of 1951. This view is from the summer of 1958, after removal of the track and looking towards Kington. In the 'Railway Mania' period of the mid–1840s, there were plans for a railway from Worcester to Aberystwyth to pass this way, and the K&ER had visions of extending west from New Radnor to Rhayader and Aberystwyth. Even as late as 1910 the *Railway Magazine* speculated persistently on extending the railway to the west; and while it was acknowledged that much engineering work and steep gradients would be involved, the port of Fishguard was by then considered the prize. The routes to cause such excitement ran from Goodwick to Newcastle Emlyn, a loop at Llandyssul, and a new line from between Lampeter and Tregaron across to New Radnor. The latter was seen as a rival to the existing GWR route from Fishguard to the Midlands; Llandrindod Wells and Aberystwyth were also mentioned in this article. The much hoped-for railway came to nothing, however.

BRITISH RAILWAYS — WESTERN REGION

INSTRUCTIONS IN REGARD TO THE USE OF THE ALARM BELLS FIXED IN THE GROUND FRAME AT BITTERLEY AND IN THE DRUM HOUSE AT CLEE HILL TOP.

An alarm bell is fixed in the ground frame at Bitterley actuated by a plunger in the Drum House at Clee Hill Top.

In the event of a trip breaking away and running down the incline or getting out of the control of the man in charge of the drum, he must depress the plunger which will cause the warning bell to ring and indicate to the pointsman at Bitterley that a runaway has occurred.

On hearing the bell ring, the pointsman at Bitterley must be on the alert and take steps to deal with the runaway by opening the trap points provided for the purpose of derailing the wagons.

Another Alarm Bell is fixed in the Drum House at Clee Hill Top for the purpose of stopping a trip of wagons proceeding down the incline, in case of emergency. The bell is rung by means of plungers one being fixed in the ground frame at Bitterley, and another on a post close to the lever at the trap points at the top of the incline.

Should anything occur which renders it desirable to stop a trip of wagons from proceeding down the incline the pointsman at Bitterley or the man at the trap points at the top of the incline as the case may be must push in the plunger on the instrument provided for the purpose of attracting the attention of the man in the Drum House.

The instruments must be tested each morning before the first trip is run. The man in charge of the cabin at the top must arrange with the man at Bitterley the time the test shall be made, and they must confirm to each other that both bells are in good order.

For the purpose of the test the plunger must be pushed in once only at each place.

The bells must not be used for any other purposes than those outlined above.

.... 1953. ....

Chester. *District Operating Superintendent.*

Above and opposite, below: In my second book for Fonthill Media, *The Last Years of Steam in Shropshire & The Severn Valley*, the wire-rope-worked Clee Hill Incline—one of Shropshire's railway curiosities—was covered in some detail. Connecting to this incline was the Clee Hill branch from Ludlow, and the black and white view is of the branch junction with the main line, together with exchange sidings in the distance. This was photographed from a Craven Arms to Hereford service on 11 October 1962 (and the date of the ticket), the actual junction being some 400 yards north of Ludlow station. The branch was built by the Ludlow & Clee Hill Railway, which obtained its Act in 1861, and the junction here was managed by the Shrewsbury & Hereford Railway, which recovered the costs from the LCHR. The branch was worked by the GWR and LNWR following an 1877 agreement, and it was vested jointly in these two companies as of 1 January 1893. By 1959, the service along the branch ran only on Mondays, Wednesdays, and Fridays, and departing from Ludlow at 11.00 a.m. The incline itself was last used in 1960, but the section from Clee Hill Junction to Bitterley, at the bottom of the incline, remained open until formal closure at the end of 1962. The instructions for the use of alarm bells on the incline were discovered in the derelict signal box at Bitterley after closure of the line by the author and his father.

BRITISH RLYS (W)   BRITISH RLYS (W)
Builth Road   Builth Road
HIGH LEVEL   HIGH LEVEL
                TO
        CRAVEN ARMS & Stokesay
             (Via Knighton)
            THIRD CLASS
          09ZZ Fare 6/11Z
Craven A.&S.   Craven A.&S.
FOR CONDITIONS   FOR CONDITIONS
SEE BACK W.D   SEE BACK W.D

Above: Monday 15 June 1964 saw a number of significant railway closures in Wales, together with more reductions in steam. The steam-worked route from Pontypool Road to Neath which cut across the South Wales valleys was closed to passengers. Also, the Central Wales Line from Shrewsbury to Swansea changed from steam to diesel multiple unit (DMU) operation, and this line's southern section from Pontardulais to Swansea Victoria lost its passenger service. Tuesday 26 May 1964 and the Whitsun half-term school holiday gave the opportunity for me and my father to travel over these routes with a circular tour starting from Hereford. A surprise was in store at Pontardulais; here, the pannier tank that had hauled the train from Swansea Victoria was replaced, not by the expected Black 5, but with the now-preserved Jubilee No. 45699 *Galatea*. This is the scene at Craven Arms as No. 45699 prepares to depart on the final leg of its journey to Shrewsbury. (If you would like to hear No. 45699 departing on the train in this photograph, then visit the author's website, michaelclemensrailways.co.uk. In the 'Sound Bites' section are a selection of freely downloadable railway tape recordings from the 1960s which include *Galatea* departing from Craven Arms.) The date on the ticket is unclear, but appears to be 30 October 1958.

Below and opposite below: Another circular railway trip from Hereford, but not with the author, took place on Thursday 11 October 1962 (the date of the ticket). This time the journey was via Three Cocks Junction, Builth Road, and Craven Arms. The first view is taken just after leaving Knighton on the way to Craven Arms. The locomotive shed is on the left, and this remained in use until January 1962 for banking duties with the quite heavy freight traffic up the single-track, 1-in-60 gradient towards Llangunllo. After this, the banking locomotive was supplied from Craven Arms shed, and on 11 October it was the now-preserved No. 3205, which left Craven Arms at 3.40 a.m. and returned as required in the late evening. The signal box in the distance is Knighton No. 1: it had opened in 1871, but was replaced by this new box in June 1906. Between Knighton No. 2 signal box and Craven Arms was double track (there since the early 1870s) with a speed restriction of 55 mph. The impressive and well guyed LNWR signal array at Hopton Heath is seen on departure in the second photograph. This includes a co-acting example: these duplicate signals were used where sighting was adversely affected by curvature, an intervening overbridge, or station canopy, for instance. Following the cessation of through-freight traffic on 10 August 1964, there was no real need for the double-track, and on Sunday 12 December 1965 this was removed and a single line section was created all the way from Craven Arms to Llandrindod Wells.

1965 was the last year that the GWR *Manor*-class 4-6-0s worked from Shrewsbury to the Welsh coast; in fact, it was the last full year that any class of GWR 4-6-0 remained in service at all. This is again Shrewsbury, and No. 7821 *Ditcheat Manor* is waiting in one of the bay platforms before taking out the down Cambrian Coast Express, the date is believed to be 26 August 1965. Looking back, it is astonishing to think that a locomotive in such an outwardly decrepit condition, seemingly one step removed from the scrap yard, would be expected to work the premier express passenger service from Shrewsbury to Aberystwyth. The GWR curved nameplates had already become something of a collector's item, and anticipating possible theft, the authorities removed them from the beginning of 1965 for safekeeping—even today, these nameplates sell for thousands of pounds. The now nameless No. 7821 has just the three fixing brackets for the nameplate remaining over its centre coupled wheel. It is also missing the cab-side number plate and shed plate, but has a painted 2B (Wolverhampton Oxley) shed code instead. Two tape recordings of No. 7821 on this day are freely downloadable from the author's website.

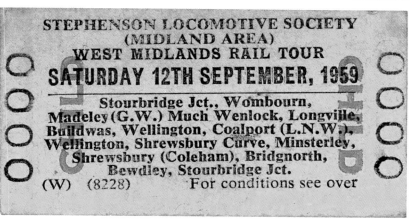

STEPHENSON LOCOMOTIVE SOCIETY
(MIDLAND AREA)
WEST MIDLANDS RAIL TOUR
SATURDAY 12TH SEPTEMBER, 1959

Stourbridge Jct., Wombourn,
Madeley (G.W.) Much Wenlock, Longville,
Buildwas, Wellington, Coalport (L.N.W.),
Wellington, Shrewsbury Curve, Minsterley,
Shrewsbury (Coleham), Bridgnorth,
Bewdley, Stourbridge Jct.
(W) (8228)   For conditions see over

Opposite and above: As we now head west from Shrewsbury following in the tracks of the Cambrian Coast Express, branching southwards was the railway to Minsterley. As with many rural lines, there were hopes that it might be extended beyond the small town of Minsterley. It featured in proposals over the years to places such as Newtown and onwards to Aberystwyth via Llangurig, and an extension to the Bishops Castle Railway - but they all came to nothing. The first photograph shows the SLS 'West Midlands' rail tour of Saturday 12 September 1959, with its DMU standing at a derelict-looking Minsterley Station; it had lost its regular passenger service in 1951, although freight continued until 1967. Note the three intrepid (or should that be foolhardy) enthusiasts risking their lives in pursuit of a good photograph from the top of the water tower. The Minsterley branch also connected with the narrow-gauge Snailbeach District Railways at Pontesbury and this is seen in the undated second photograph. After 1947 this line was operated by Shropshire County Council, and instead of using a 'normal' locomotive they worked the line with a Fordson tractor transporting granite for use in road-building, and the tractor is just visible in the distance. In 1959 road access was provided to the quarry and the line fell out of use, the final lengths of rail being lifted in 1962. (*The above is from Alan Maund's collection*)

A great friend of myself and my father was Dennis Bath from Worcester, and at Christmas, cards would be exchanged based on a railway theme of some kind. This is one such card from Dennis. Although no details were included, it is obviously a view of a busy time at Welshpool Station, looking north from the B4381 road bridge. Churchward 2-6-0 No. 5369 is displaying an 84E (Tyseley Birmingham) shed code and the outside steam pipes which were fitted to it in September 1956. It was transferred to 82B (St Philip's Marsh, Bristol) in November 1960. The working concerned is probably one of the summer Saturdays-only through-services from Birmingham to the Welsh coast. In the summer of 1959 there were two such workings, one to Aberystwyth and the other to Barmouth. The other three locomotives consist of two Collett-2251-class 0-6-0s plus another Churchward 2-6-0 (the furthest away). The only number out of these three that can be resolved is that of No. 2217; this was allocated to Machynlleth shed from the mid–1950s until 1962. It is still possible to stand on this road bridge today, but the view is rather different. The main station building survives but is not rail connected, and the modern-day track approximately follows that on which No. 2217 is standing to a new Welshpool Station in the distance. The track on which No. 5369 is standing is nowadays part of the A483 road, the Welshpool by-pass. (*Dennis Bath's collection*)

The B4381 road bridge from which the opposite photograph was taken is in the background, as No. 7803 *Barcote Manor* draws in to Welshpool Station during, what is believed to be, the early part of January 1965. The service concerned is the up Cambrian Coast Express to London Paddington, and this consisted of two separate parts—one from Pwllheli and one from Aberystwyth—which were joined together at Dovey Junction for the onward journey. The *Railway Observer* reported that, at this time, Aberystwyth shed diagrammed both Nos 7802 and 7803 to the Cambrian Coast Express, and kept them both in immaculate condition. But this rather pampered treatment did not last for much longer, as both locomotives were transferred in January 1965 to Shrewsbury shed. Although the first *Manors* were built in 1938, economy was practised with their tenders and many ran with examples dating from between about 1910 and 1915. However, as of January 1961 No. 7803 ran with this visibly larger intermediate-type tender. (*Alan Maund's collection*)

The Welshpool & Llanfair Light Railway began within the standard-gauge goods yard at Welshpool, and on leaving a 5-mph speed restriction applied for the first of the 9 miles and 4 chains to Llanfair Caereinion. Trains climbed over the Shropshire Union Canal and then halted for the crossing of Church Street, as seen in the above photograph. This site is still recognisable today, with St Mary's Church in the background. No. 822 is heading westwards with what appears to be a trainload of coal, all of which will have had to be manually transhipped from standard-gauge wagons. The date of both photographs is Friday 6 April 1956. Next, the train was carried over the Sylfaen Brook on a continuous bridge, and threaded its way through the narrow passage between the houses—and washing! This section largely followed the course of an earlier horse-drawn tramway—the Welsh Pool Rail Road—that had connected to the Montgomeryshire Canal but was abandoned by 1854. When the W&L was preserved, Welshpool Borough Council decided that trains would not be allowed to work over this town section, so today the heritage railway starts from its Raven Square Station on the outskirts of the town. The last train ran over the town section on 17 August 1963. (*Dennis Bath's collection*)

Your author went with his late father on railway visits all over Britain from a very young age, and of course got to know his father's pals. A great friend was Dennis Bath, and when your author was just six years of age he was presented by Dennis with three framed photographs of the W&L, and all will appear over the next few pages. The first is another taken on 6 April 1956 with No. 822 hauling the Llanfair Caereinion-bound freight train, as seen previously crossing Church Street in Welshpool. This is believed to be where the W&L followed the north side of Brook Street (Welshpool) on a wide verge, near the Standard Quarry, before reaching Raven Square. The building in the background appears to be nameboarded, 'The Salvation Army'. The 5-mph speed limit mentioned at Church Street also applied along Brook Street and all the way to Raven Square, after which it increased to its maximum of 15 mph. Throughout the years of the passenger service—which ceased in 1931—the maximum speed on the branch was 25 mph. (*Dennis Bath's collection*)

W&L services needed to be extremely cautious when crossing the main Welshpool–Llanfair Caereinion road (A458) as it was unprotected. This is Raven Square and it is adjacent to the crossing, nowadays this area is where the new station at the eastern end of the preserved railway has been constructed. Prior to 1931 there was a Raven Square Halt, but it was on the abandoned town section. The notices visible are from the Welshpool & Llanfair Railway Preservation Society, inviting people to attend a public meeting at Raven Square on Saturday 26 September 1959. The line was leased from BR at the end of 1962 and a passenger service commenced on 6 April 1963. A problem for the preserved railway was that, although Welshpool was by far the larger town and generated custom for the line, the centre of operations was at Llanfair Caereinion. All the facilities used to be at Welshpool, but of course they became inaccessible once the town section was abandoned.

This is another of the framed photographs given to me when I was a child by Dennis Bath, taken of the same westbound freight train over the W&L with No. 822 on 6 April 1956. The location this time is the main intermediate station of Castle Caereinion, and the signal box (closed in 1931), corrugated iron waiting shelter, and passing loop are all discernible. As this book was being written, services on the preserved railway had started to pass again at Castle Caereinion; also, the road crossing (behind the photographer) is in the process of being automated following safety concerns. The line was one of the few narrow-gauge lines built under the powers of the 1896 Light Railways Act, and as a result it has limited earthworks, sharp curves, varying gradients, and level crossings rather than bridges. The coal visible here will have to have been shovelled from one gauge to the other at Welshpool, only to be shovelled out again at Llanfair Caereinion. Another 2 feet 6 inches gauge line built under the 1896 Act, the Leek & Manifold Railway in Staffordshire, used transporter wagons. Standard-gauge wagons were carried on top of specially constructed narrow-gauge wagons, thus circumventing the need for transhipment. (*Dennis Bath's collection*)

Opposite, above: There had been two earlier schemes for railways between Welshpool and Llanfair Caereinion, in the 1870s and 1880s, but they came to nothing. It was the Light Railways Act of 1896 that provided the stimulus for the line actually built. A condition of the Light Railway Order obtained on 8 September 1899 was that the W&L had to be worked by an existing company, and accordingly an agreement was made with the CR for ninety-nine years, the CR to receive 60 per cent of gross receipts. The final photograph of the W&L taken by Dennis Bath is also the earliest: this is a special train organised for the Railway Development Association on 12 September 1953. The tour had begun from Birmingham Snow Hill using a GWR railcar and reached Welshpool via Shifnal, but returned via the Severn Valley line and Bewdley. The special on the W&L consisted of four open wagons and two brake vans hauled by No. 823, seen here on the return to Welshpool taking water shortly after leaving Llanfair Caereinion. Page 6 of the Introduction contains an early preservation era photograph of this same water tank. (*Dennis Bath's collection*)

Below: Back to the standard-gauge, as we now head west along the CR from Welshpool. This is believed to be another photograph dating from early January 1965, with No. 7803 *Barcote Manor* on the down Cambrian Coast Express just after leaving Welshpool and crossing the River Severn. The photograph was taken from the adjacent A490 road and very close by Cilcewydd Mill, a former Victorian corn mill powered by water turbines. This may well have been photographed on the same day as the earlier picture in this book of No. 7803 coming in to Welshpool on the up Cambrian Coast Express (page 57). Authorisation was given to the Oswestry & Newtown Railway in 1855 and the line was opened between Welshpool and Abermule on 10 June 1861. The section of track here was doubled in 1925 (from Welshpool to Forden) but singled later in the 1960s, only to be doubled again recently in connection with the increase of service frequency to hourly between Shrewsbury and Aberystwyth. (*Alan Maund's collection*)

By 1966, the only year-round steam-hauled passenger trains each way between Shrewsbury and Aberystwyth were the Cambrian Coast Express and the mail train. But things were different on summer Saturdays, when extra long-distance trains were run for the benefit of holidaymakers to and from Manchester, Birmingham, and London. Although there was a reduction in the number of holidaymakers travelling by rail, this was counterbalanced by the fact that other lines to the Cambrian coast, such as that from Ruabon to Barmouth, had been closed—so the remaining traffic was concentrated on this one route. Both views are at Montgomery Station on Saturday 20 August 1966. Firstly, No. 76038 is entering the station double-heading a service to the coast; the bracketed signal behind shows that it was possible to run down services through the up platform. This strategy allowed the signal box to be switched out (closed), and was useful on Sundays when there was often just one train each way. In my previous book for Fonthill Media, *The Last Years of Steam in Shropshire and the Severn Valley*, No. 76038 appears in a line of scrap locomotives at Shrewsbury in October 1966. At the other end of the station and again heading west is No. 75047. Montgomery Station had closed on 14 June 1965, as had many of the stations between Welshpool and Aberystwyth. (*Alan Maund's collection*)

Another two photographs that date from Saturday 20 August 1966, both of which are thought to have been taken between Montgomery and Abermule. The first, displaying the correct lamp head code for a breakdown train not in service, is of an unidentified BR-class 78xxx lightweight 2-6-0 heading towards Newtown. Shrewsbury shed had seven of this class around this time, and when not in store they were often used on the thrice-weekly Minsterley branch freight, plus daily workings to Oswestry which included the quarries around Porthywaen (often double-heading back to Shrewsbury with the stone trains). The class were also used for shunting duties around the county town, such as at Coton Hill goods yard, Abbey (S&M) Station, and Hookagate permanent way depot. In the second photograph, heading towards Welshpool is an unidentified-class 75xxx lightweight 4-6-0. It is hauling nine coaches, so almost certainly will have needed assistance in climbing up Talerddig Bank. In April 1965, Machynlleth and Shrewsbury sheds between them had six of this class, but after the withdrawal of all the GW *Manors* by the end of 1965, the numbers of the 75xxxs increased. For the summer of 1966, even more arrived following a deliberate policy to allow for double-heading to improve timekeeping. Even as late as November 1966, and taking into account withdrawals, there were still fourteen examples between the two sheds. (*Alan Maund's collection*)

Abermule was the next station westwards after Montgomery, and the scene of a terrible head-on collision in 1921 in which seventeen people were killed. The view in the first photograph faces east from the up platform on 23 March 1959. Dennis Bath, Eric Parker, and my father were waiting for the 9.20 a.m. all-stations service to Aberystwyth. They were about to start on a 196-mile-long rail tour across Central Wales, and we have already seen one of the concluding photographs of that day, taken at Brecon (page 16). The signal box controlled the level crossing of the B4368 and so, unlike Montgomery, could not be switched out on a Sunday. Instead it opened for the down train at 7.00 a.m. and again at 7.45 p.m. for the up train. Curving away to the right from the far side of the down platform is what was left of the branch to Kerry. The soon-to-be-retiring station master is by the crossing gates; he had tried to buy land on the site of the branch to build a property, as he would shortly have to vacate his railway house. The branch to Kerry had opened in 1863 but lost its passenger service by 1931; it closed altogether on 1 May 1956. The branch was dismantled three years later, and the second photograph is of Kerry Station in August 1959.

An up working is pulling away from Newtown Station on Saturday 7 August 1965, hauled by an unidentified-class 75xxx in this view taken from next to the A489 road bridge. I used to find it difficult to tell a 75xxx from a 76xxx in a head-on view such as this one, where the wheels or locomotive number cannot really be seen. A difference, and barely visible, is in the steeply-sloping running plate between the buffer-beam and the level running-board section along the side of the boiler—the 75xxxs have only one step, whereas the 76xxxs have two. The reporting code on the locomotive is sadly illegible, but with only three coaches it would seem unlikely to be a summer Saturdays-only holidaymaker's service, and it certainly is not the Cambrian Coast Express or the mail train. Perhaps it is a steam replacement for one of the, by this time, DMU-hauled Aberystwyth to Shrewsbury trains. The local stopping service at thirteen of the more rural stations between Welshpool and Aberystwyth had been withdrawn with the introduction of the summer timetable in June 1965. (*Alan Maund's collection*)

In the 1850s both Newtown (population 4,000) and Llanidloes (population 4,500) were prosperous boroughs. An 1852 scheme—later modified with LNWR backing—would have built a railway from Shrewsbury to Aberystwyth that passed through Newtown, but not the larger town of Llanidloes, as had originally been planned. The incensed residents of Llanidloes set about financing and building their own railway to connect with the 1852 proposal at Newtown, and this became Montgomeryshire's first railway—the Llanidloes & Newtown Railway that was incorporated in 1853. Ironically, the 1852 LNWR-backed scheme failed to pass through the Commons, and the L&N was, quite unintentionally, created in grand isolation. The L&N station was at the western end of Newtown some way from the town centre, and it opened fully on 31 August 1859. The second of Montgomeryshire's railways to be built was the Oswestry & Newtown Railway, and both the L&N and O&N agreed in September 1859 on a new joint station at Newtown, nearer the town centre. After this opened, the original terminus platform was used as a coal wharf, its building becoming the coal merchant's office. This is the joint station, seen on 9 June 1966 facing east. The large building behind it, and bearing an 1895 date on it, was the headquarters of the pioneering mail-order business established by Welsh entrepreneur Sir Pryce Pryce-Jones. It was Britain's first large-scale mail-order business, the nearby railway ensuring a prompt dispatch to customers around the world, and which included Queen Victoria and Florence Nightingale.

Moat Lane Junction was on the main line from Welshpool to Aberystwyth and gave connection to a north–south route that passed through the heart of Mid-Wales. There was no town of Moat Lane; it was simply a place to change trains. The first line passing through was the L&N opened in 1859, although there was no station on this site until 1863, when the line to Machynlleth opened. The L&N can just be made out to the right of the Moat Lane East signal box, looking towards Newtown on 4 October 1962. No. 7819 *Hinton Manor* is taking water during its wait here at about 4.20 p.m. while working the afternoon Aberystwyth to Oswestry stopping service. Despite being the more important line, the one from Machynlleth curves round to join the straight route from Llanidloes because the L&N tracks were the first here. Even non-stopping services from Machynlleth had to slow to 25 mph. There was double-track from the Moat Lane West signal box for the 4 miles and 55 chains to Newtown, the section onwards to Newtown being converted from single-track in 1912. The coal wagons by the water tower are for the pump house, and when this was under repair in late 1954, a withdrawn ex-Taff Vale Railway locomotive was brought in as a replacement stationary boiler.

The locomotive shed at Moat Lane was situated between the diverging Machynlleth and Llanidloes lines, with access only from the Machynlleth route. The original shed was blown down in 1955, and this is the 1957-built replacement, seen from an Aberystwyth-bound train on 23 March 1959. It was erected on the same site, but was a completely new, corrugated shed with a single-pitch roof measuring 35 feet by 70 feet. Noted at Moat Lane on this day were Nos 46526 and 78005. The line to Llanidloes runs from left to right behind the shed, the station to the left. By late 1953, Ivatt 2-6-0s had taken over many of the workings on the Mid-Wales Line, of which ten were allocated to Brecon, three of these stabled overnight at Moat Lane. Work had shrunk considerably since the Second World War, as in 1939 it had turns for seven or eight locomotives. In 1923 it was proposed to move the locomotive department to the south side of the Llanidloes line, but this came to nothing, as also happened with a couple more schemes in the early 1950s. The engine shed closed at the same time as the junction station, on 31 December 1962. On 4 October 1962, the bay platform at Moat Lane Junction plays host to these old clerestory coaches being used by the engineering department.

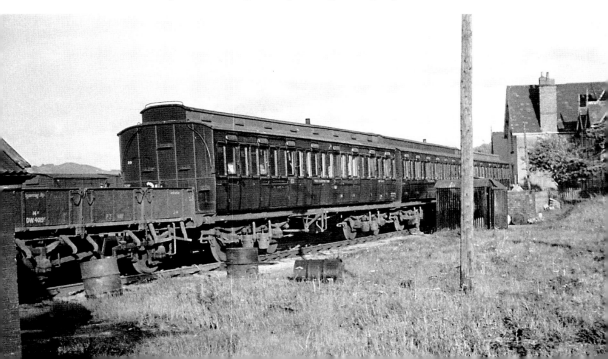

The clerestory coaches seen in the black and white view previously are now on the right of this colour photograph taken on the same day, Thursday 4 October 1962. It is about 4.30 p.m., and No. 78002—a Machynlleth-allocated locomotive since May 1953—is making its way back home on a stopping service from Newtown. On the far side of the island platform is No. 46516, and this will work the 5.30 p.m. service to Builth Wells in the next picture. Despite its rather secluded location, Moat Lane Junction did have a refreshment room, and as with Talyllyn Junction seen earlier, it was not operated by British Transport Catering Services. The pump house must be working today, as smoke can be seen rising above the first coach behind No. 46516. Services still stopped here after closure at the end of 1962 for water. Indeed, I myself stopped here behind No. 80132 on 2 January 1964, when travelling from Dovey Junction to Oswestry. This was a class notorious for concerns over its water capacity. The design of the 1952-introduced BR Class 2 2-6-0 (No. 78002) very closely resembled that of the 1946-introduced LMS Ivatt Class 2 2-6-0 (No. 46516). The main things your author used to tell the difference between the two head-on, apart from the number, were: that the BR version had a sloping plate from the low running-board to the buffer-beam, thus covering the cylinders, whereas this was left open on the Ivatt version; also, that the BR version had smaller cab spectacle-windows.

No. 46516 has now made it over to the Llanidloes line platform at Moat Lane Junction on 4 October 1962, and is standing ready to work the 5.30 p.m. to Llanidloes, Rhayader, and Builth Wells. Strangely, the ticket is dated 5 October 1962. From new this locomotive had spent its entire life at either Oswestry or Brecon sheds, but on closure of Oswestry shed in January 1965 it went to Speke Junction (Liverpool) and was withdrawn form Northwich in May 1967. The original (L&N) Moat Lane Station was situated a few hundred yards towards Llanidloes, and was built to serve nearby Caersws, but this was closed in 1863 when a station on the newly-built line to Machynlleth was actually opened at Caersws. An Amalgamation Bill of 1864 merged together the L&N, the O&N, the Newtown & Machynlleth, and the Oswestry, Ellesmere & Whitchurch Railways, into the Cambrian Railways (the plural used in preliminary negotiations enduring). But we will now branch off the main line we have followed westwards towards the coast, and instead follow No. 46516 along the Mid-Wales Line; this was initially seen as 'a rich vision', but it proved to be something of 'a weak reality'.

2nd-SINGLE   SINGLE-2nd

0256   0256

Moat Lane to

Moat Lane
Builth Wells

Moat Lane
Builth Wells

BUILTH WELLS

Via Llanidloes

(W)   8/6   Fare   8/6   (W)

For conditions see over   For conditions see over

Taken from the lunchtime Brecon to Moat Lane Junction through-service departing from Llanidloes on 4 October 1962 (and also the date of the ticket), this is a view of the island platform. Waiting to depart about half an hour later and following in our tracks is an Ivatt Class 2 2-6-0 on the school train to Moat Lane Junction; on Saturdays and school holidays, this ran empty and non-stop. In the afterglow of the 'Railway Mania' in the 1840s, Llanidloes was for a number of years very much in the forefront as regards railway schemes. Proposals seemingly went to all points of the compass—Manchester, Shrewsbury, Aberystwyth, Milford, and Brecon. Yet Llanidloes ended up as a merely intermediate station, on something of a rural backwater between Moat Lane Junction and Brecon. When the passenger services ceased at the end of 1962, the Transport Users' Consultative Committee (TUCC) favoured retaining the link to Moat Lane for freight only. This done, it got a new lease on life when work began on the Clywedog Dam in the hills 3 miles from Llanidloes. Cement trains from Aberthaw in South Wales by then had to travel via Shrewsbury to Llanidloes, the direct route via Talyllyn Junction and Rhayader having been shut down of course. The cement traffic kept the line going for a while, but total closure ensued on 2 October 1967.

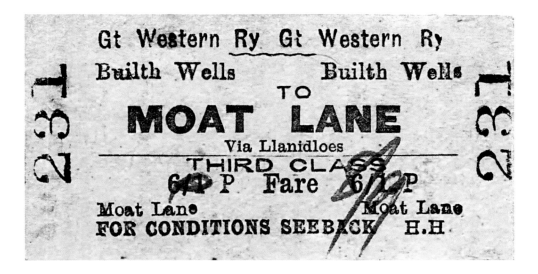

The most famous, or arguably *in*famous plan for a strategic route through Llanidloes was the original Manchester & Milford Railway proposal of 1845. This company had eighty-six directors and a grandiloquent prospectus, the idea was to use the West Wales port for the import and export of Lancashire's raw materials and goods. The plan was revived in both the 1850s and 1860s. Reaching Llanidloes from the Manchester direction was not too great a challenge, and reasonably level following the River Severn for the previous 30 miles or so. But west of Llanidloes was a different matter: the mountainous and steeply graded 20 miles to Strata Florida involved 1½ miles of tunnelling plus a viaduct 280 feet high. The only part of the mountain section actually built was that visible on the embankment heading off to the left as far as Llangurig, and only a short distance away. The M&MR and the Mid-Wales Railway came together here at Penpontbren Junction. Only one freight train ever made it to Llangurig, and that for legal rather than commercial reasons. By then the money had run out, and the line was lifted as long ago as 1882. The whole idea of the M&MR seemed rather absurd, Liverpool being a far more convenient port. I have always been rather intrigued by one of the grounds put forward for its failure—the American Civil War!—and the subsequent major disruption of raw cotton deliveries to Lancashire. This photograph is looking north from the rear of a Builth Wells-bound train on 4 October 1962.

Above and opposite below: These views are of Rhayader Station, taken on 13 December 1962. This is the same up train on the same day as seen earlier at Talyllyn Junction (page 18): my father had followed its progress up the Mid-Wales Line as far as Rhayader. The town is situated on the A44 main road, and this allowed an easy drive home, as the family house in Pershore (Worcestershire) was also on the A44. This signal box had opened in 1891; in fact, there had been much activity around Rhayader at this time in connection with the building of the original Elan Valley Dams. The goods sidings on the right were multiplied, and a dedicated railway was built to the south of Rhayader that connected to the works. History was repeated when the Claerwen Dam was built after the Second World War. Although the waterworks branch was long-closed, cement was brought in by dedicated trains to Rhayader. The 1949 working timetable shows this arriving every weekday at 10.45 p.m. having left Talyllyn Junction at 9.10 p.m., the locomotive and brake van then working back to Builth Wells shed and arriving there at 11.35 p.m. The empty 'containers' left Rhayader at 5.25 p.m., the locomotive and brake van coming up from Builth Wells first. After closure of the line at the end of 1962, Rhayader Station was retained as a non-rail connected depot until 5 April 1965, for coal only.

Two more photographs at Rhayader Station taken on 13 December 1962, also the date of the ticket. The desire to exploit the completion of the Vale of Towy Railway from Llandilo to Llandovery in 1858, and thus give access to Llanelly and Milford, led to the railway being built through Rhayader. It was planned to run from Llanidloes through Rhayader, Newbridge-on-Wye, and Llanwrtyd to Llandovery. But a competitor backed by the LNWR planned a line from Knighton to Llandovery. From Builth to Llandovery, the two routes ran parallel, and they went before a Commons committee on 16 March 1859. The eventually winner was the LNWR route, the Rhayader proposal being cut short at Newbridge. So the company refocused and looked instead towards the industrial riches of Merthyr Tydfil and the South Wales valleys, and thus was conceived the Mid-Wales Railway on 1 August 1859. But even here the Mid-Wales Railway was frustrated, the Brecon & Merthyr Railway was incorporated on the same day and blocked the natural approach route from Central to South Wales— the 'rich vision' was turning sour. In these images, the unidentified Ivatt Class 2 at the down platform will have passed the up service seen previously at Pantydwr, the only crossing point by now between Rhayader and Llanidloes. In the distance is a Cambrian-type signal, but the decorative and substantial water column was a Mid-Wales type, with a fire devil to its side to stop it freezing.

So now the MWR had to build its railway, and although this didn't involve the extensive tunnelling and high viaduct of the M&MR, it did involve climbing to 947 feet at Pantydwr—considerably higher than the more famous Central Wales summit of Talerddig. It also involved two tunnels at Marteg (372 yards) and Rhayader (268 yards). As described in the previous commentary, the MWR became involved in battles over access, but in many ways the fiercest was over the approach to Brecon. Also, the early promise of coal traffic to Birkenhead from South Wales faded away, it being resisted by other companies, while the use of coastal shipping struck another blow. The MWR really was left with a 'weak reality'. Rescue came when the CR took over the working of the MWR in an agreement dated 29 February 1888 (a leap year). This proved a success and steps were made to prepare for an amalgamation, effective on 1 July 1904. Newbridge-on-Wye is seen on a sunny but cold afternoon on 13 December 1962, just before 3.00 p.m.; again, No. 46511 is making its way slowly up the Mid-Wales Line to Moat Lane Junction from Brecon. The station had staggered platforms and the signal box on the down platform dated from June 1891; the siding on the far right gave access to the cattle pens.

This view is looking north up the old MWR towards Newbridge-on-Wye, and seen from the LNWR line to South Wales at Builth Road (High Level). The date is 11 October 1962, and the film Perutz. When the MWR had aspirations of reaching Llandovery, both it and the competing LNWR (Central Wales Extension) followed similar routes from here. A connection was agreed between the two on 30 June 1864, in the form of a 483-yard-long spur laid in the direction of the MWR's original objective, Llandovery. The spur, seen branching off to the left in the middle distance and in front of the row of terraced houses, was brought into use on 1 November 1866. Exchange sidings were also built on the spur, as was an engine shed. These houses, called 'Wye View Terrace', were built for railway workers and their families. I recall seeing this spur used as a refuge siding for a Shrewsbury-bound freight train when I passed through Builth Road (High Level) on 26 May 1964. Of course, at this time there could be no exchange of traffic, as the MWR line had been shut since December 1962. The signal box visible on the right by the junction with the connecting spur is Builth Road (Low Level)—previous to 1935 this had been called Builth Road North—and in 1959 the box opened at 5.45 a.m. The siding on the left and partly in shadow is the Builth Road shunting neck, a refuge siding with a capacity of twenty-four wagons.

The station at Builth Road (Low Level) is seen in both of these views, the monochrome photograph dating from the early summer of 1958 (the same day as that taken at New Radnor on page 48). The colour view is another from 13 December 1962, with No. 46511 in the up platform, my father having parked the family maroon Vauxhall just outside the station. The path to the High Level can be seen in the colour view, and also a glimpse of the lift between the two levels. The station, initially built without a passing loop, was opened by the MWR in 1864 (goods on 1 September, and passengers on 21 September) in anticipation of the arrival of the Central Wales Line in 1866. It was at first called Llechryd, becoming Builth Road in 1899, and the Low Level was added in 1950. The station had the refinement of gas lighting, the crossing loop and up platform were both added by 1893, but the south signal box that used to exist at the end of the down platform closed in 1935. All the MWR main and junction stations were built of stone, but none had roofed platforms. All later had refreshment rooms, and latterly the one here was privately operated instead of by British Transport Catering Services, and it still survives today as the Cambrian Arms.

With the GWR already well established around Swansea, it can be appreciated just how anxious the LNWR were to complete their own route from Craven Arms to the industrial riches of this area. By 1889, the LNWR owned, jointly owned, or had running powers over the 95 miles and 48 chains to Swansea Victoria Station. All the LNWR-owned lines passed to the LMS at the grouping, but at nationalisation in 1948, everything passed to the Western Region of BR. Both photographs were taken at Builth Road (High Level) Station: it was 37 miles and 40 chains from Craven Arms and marked the boundary between the Chester and Swansea Districts. The first is of Black Five No. 45283 entering from Swansea on 30 October 1958; behind it is the lift built in 1887 for transfers between the two stations, and behind that the steam of an Ivatt Class 2 my father had travelled up on. The second view is of the up platform and buildings, and taken from close by the lift on 5 January 1961. This station opened in 1866 as plain old 'Builth Road', the up loop was opened in 1868, and the High Level was added in 1950. In connection with the rationalisation of the line's infrastructure, the up side of the loop was taken out of use in October 1965.

The up track through the station here at Llandrindod Wells was taken out of use in December 1955, at which time the No. 2 signal box on the down platform was also closed. Services could still pass at Llandrindod Wells, but only outside the station on the section doubled in May 1876 and which continued to the next station of Penybont. In this undated photograph, Stanier 8F No. 48354 is making its way with a freight service from South West Wales to England. This locomotive had spent many years at Shrewsbury shed, so would be no stranger to Llandrindod Wells. It was transferred to Northampton in September 1964, coinciding with the withdrawal of through-freight traffic over this line the previous month. A local freight service initially carried on, though, and operated daily (Monday to Friday) between Pantyffynon and Craven Arms. It was worked by Llanelly-based 8Fs with crews from Pantyffynon and Craven Arms, the locomotive stabling overnight in Craven Arms shed and the crews changing over at Builth Road, where the services were booked to pass. This local freight traffic was fairly extensive from Pantyffynon to Llandrindod Wells, but meagre further on to Craven Arms. After 1 March 1965, when both Broome and Knighton lost their freight facilities, it called only at Bucknell as required. By the summer of 1965, the local freight service was only operating from Llandilo Junction (Llanelly) to Llandrindod Wells, and by then with an English Electric Type 3 diesel. The ticket is dated 26 May 1964. (*M. Roberts, Kidderminster Railway Museum*)

2nd - SPECIAL CHEAP DAY	SPECIAL - 2nd CHEAP DAY
Llandrindod Wells to	Swansea Victoria to
SWANSEA VICTORIA	LLANDRINDOD WELLS
via Llandovery	via Llandovery
(W)	(W)
For conditions see over	For conditions see over

0384 0384

Cynghordy Station, situated in the middle of a nearly 9-mile-long single-track climb from Llandovery to Sugar Loaf Summit. Over 4 miles of this climb were at a grade of 1 in 60, and there was just the one platform at Cynghordy, on the down side. An 8F is passing through on 5 June 1963, towards Llandovery. The loop and signal box were opened in July 1929 and bi-directional running was possible on both tracks; however, two passenger trains were not allowed to pass at Cynghordy. The loop was taken out of use and the signal box closed at the beginning of August 1965 in the gradual rundown of the entire route. As recently as 1960, expenditure of £676,000 had been approved to introduce Centralised Traffic Control (CTC) over the 60 miles between Craven Arms and Llandovery. CTC had originated in the USA and could most effectively increase a line's capacity. A single CTC signal box at Llandrindod Wells would have eliminated eighteen conventional signal boxes, and the line would have been continuously track-circuited with colour-light signalling, together with the installation of lifting barriers at certain level crossings. The reason for all this was expected industrial development in South Wales, such as the steel works at Margam (Port Talbot) and Llanwern (Newport), plus the NCB at Cynheidre Colliery—it was thought the capacity of existing routes would be taxed. Interestingly, the considerable rail-based oil traffic that did develop in the mid–1960s from Milford Haven and Llandarcy (Swansea) didn't receive a mention. But at the end of the day, it was found that everything could be accommodated on the still open line from Swansea to Cardiff and Newport, and the CTC proposal for the Central Wales Line was abandoned. (*F.G. Wood, Kindderminster Railway Museum*)

After the MWR dropped down to the Wye Valley at Marteg, for the next 30 miles or so it was relatively easy-going, but it did involve bridging the Wye a number of times. These two photographs of northbound services following the river date from the last months of the line at the end of 1962. Something that has always puzzled me is the building of these new Ivatt Class 2s in the early 1950s, especially for this route. Surely the well-proven GWR railcars, particularly the type introduced at the beginning of the Second World War, or a development of them, would have been a better choice for such rural services? When all the 'Four Ways to Brecon' did close, 350 railwaymen lost their jobs in an area where they were hard to get—forty alone were put out of work at Llanidloes. The TUCC estimated that the replacement bus services would cost only 7 per cent of the savings realised, but the substitute buses proved inadequate. Among others, Rhayader District Council complained, as did councillors at Llanidloes, and the *Liverpool Post* highlighted the problem. The result was that the Moat Lane to Brecon replacement bus service went back to the TUCC in 1964. Coach services from Liverpool to Cardiff and Newtown to Cardiff were introduced in July 1964, and a revised bus service started in September 1964. One benefit was that when more railway closures were proposed in Central Wales for 1964–65, the hard-learnt lessons of substitute bus services along the old MWR had been taken to heart.

As we resume our journey westwards from Moat Lane Junction, it will be recalled that the first station at Moat Lane, on the line to Llanidloes before the junction existed, was built to serve Caersws. This station was about 1 mile distant from the village, and was closed in 1863. The Caersws Station still open today was the creation of the Newtown & Machynlleth Railway in 1863; however, this photograph and commentary concern the third station to serve Caersws, built by the Van Railway. This railway was built privately without an Act and was first registered on 9 June 1870; it served lead mines on the eastern slopes of Plynlimon, which had seen their share price jump from £4 10s to £86 each in 1869. The first goods trains ran in August 1871 and the passenger service started in December 1873. Although at first around 1,000 people worked in the mines, few passengers were attracted to the VR, and by 1879 total annual passenger revenue came to only £31. At Caersws the VR had their own station, seen directly ahead in this photograph taken on 9 June 1966, plus there was a run-round loop. Further to the left, and only partly visible is the VR engine shed. The output of the mines ground to a halt in 1890, but by this time the CR was using the mine's spoil heaps as track ballast—it had excellent weed-killing properties. The line shut in 1893, but to maintain its source of ballast, the CR entered into an agreement to use it in 1895. The VR remained independent until absorbed by the GWR, and in its final years saw occasional goods and ballast trains; it finally closed on 4 November 1940. The track was lifted, except by the old VR Caersws Station, and this was used by the engineering department, as it still was at the time that this photograph was taken from an Aberystwyth-bound service.

These two photographs were taken at Carno on 7 August 1965. Coming up the bank (1 in 121 at this location) from Caersws is No. 7802 *Bradley Manor*, with eight coaches in the first picture. It is in typical 1965 condition and is missing its nameplate. No. 7802 had the very last 'heavy' repair of the entire *Manor* class in the summer of 1964, this including a boiler change at Swindon. Coming from the coast and looking in even worse condition is No. 7822 *Foxcote Manor*, with no smoke box number plate, or nameplate. Both locomotives were allocated to Shrewsbury in the summer of 1965, both would be withdrawn in the November, and both survived into preservation after a spell in Woodham Brothers scrap yard at Barry, South Wales. Carno Station closed from 14 June 1965, but thanks to Eric Parker's diaries the last entries in the ticket book for Saturday 12 June survive. Eighteen tickets in total were issued as follows that day: Aberdovey x 1, Aberystwyth x 3, Caersws x 2, Llanbrynmair x 1, Newtown x 7, Pontdolgoch x 2, and Shrewsbury x 2. The most expensive were the two second-class cheap-day returns to Shrewsbury at 13s 9d each; the least expensive was a child single to Pontdolgoch at 8d. Total revenue for Carno Station that day was £3 14s 11d. (*Alan Maund's collection*)

Above: Your author spent his twelfth birthday on Saturday 3 August 1963 watching the all-steam activity at and around Talerddig. At 693 feet, this was the highest point on the CR main line between Whitchurch and Aberystwyth. As can be seen from the milepost on the left, this spot was 61¼ miles from Whitchurch (Cambrian Junction). There was, and still is, a passing loop at Talerddig, by far the majority of the CR being single track. But in the steam era it was more than just a loop: it was a place where assistant locomotives helping heavy trains up the gradients from both the east and west sides were often detached, and made Talerddig a hive of activity. The time is 11.14 a.m. and No. 7823 *Hook Norton Manor* has charge of the 8.05 a.m. Birmingham Snow Hill to Barmouth summer Saturday service, and loaded to ten coaches. We had already photographed this train in Newtown Station at 10.30 a.m. on our journey from Worcestershire. No. 7823 was a Birmingham Tyseley-based locomotive at the time, and in the summer both this working and another to Aberystwyth brought the Tyseley *Manors* on to the CR. For instance, No. 7818 *Granville Manor* was seen returning home on this day with the 12.40 p.m. Aberystwyth to Birmingham Snow Hill. At the site of Moat Lane Junction Station, of course closed by now, No. 7823 had taken on water plus received banking assistance in the rear from No. 46519, seen in the next photograph.

Another summer Saturday spent watching the comings and goings at Talerddig was 13 August 1960. Sadly, as in 1963, the weather was poor with intermittent rain all day. Highlight of the day was Dukedog 4-4-0 No. 9017, only five of the class survived at the beginning of 1960, and by the August there were just two left in service. No. 9017 is acting as a pilot to No. 75020 on the 9.45 a.m. Pwllheli to London Paddington, which today is loaded to twelve coaches. This service is running about twenty minutes late and is passing No. 7822 on the eight-coach 9.45 a.m. Whitchurch to Aberystwyth train, itself about fifteen minutes late. The passing of late-running trains on single-track lines was always a problem, only complicated by the length of the loop at Talerddig—it would only hold a locomotive and ten coaches. Vigilance was required from HQ at Oswestry and neighbouring signal boxes to Talerddig to ensure that trains of exceptional length did not approach this loop at the same time. (*Dennis Bath's collection*)

Opposite: This is the view looking the other way to the previous photograph at Talerddig on 3 August 1963. The conditions were the antithesis of summer holiday weather, Eric Parker referring to this Saturday in his diary as 'a dull Novemberish day'. To the left is No. 46519, this had banked the Birmingham to Barmouth through-service loaded to ten coaches from Moat Lane Junction, and to which it was physically coupled. No. 46519 will detach itself from the train here before running back down the hill to Moat Lane Junction light engine. Coming the other way is the premier express over the route, the Cambrian Coast Express, complete with headboard—the 9.45 a.m. Aberystwyth to London Paddington. No. 7810 *Draycott Manor* is in charge today, also with ten coaches, and it has also had help up Talerddig Bank from No. 82006. This had been coupled ahead of No. 7810 acting as a pilot, and it will have pulled forward into the dead-end siding accessed from the pointwork in the foreground. Generally speaking, the assistant locomotives would uncouple and go back down the bank, and possibly might be seen again later in the day. This happened with No. 46519; it reappeared at 3.25 p.m. at the rear of the 11.05 a.m. Manchester to Aberystwyth, loaded to ten coaches and hauled by No. 80131. The ticket was used by the author after five hours of observing the proceedings at Talerddig to travel back to Newtown.

It is still Saturday 13 August 1960, but it is now 4.45 p.m. and No. 9017 is on its way back light engine to Machynlleth shed, from where it worked throughout the summer of 1960. The maximum load allowed single-handed for a *Manor* between Machynlleth and Talerddig was 288 tons tare (eight coaches), while the maximum onwards towards Shrewsbury was 336 tons tare. There are twelve coaches on the 9.45 Pwllheli to London Paddington (in the previous photograph) which the pair has hauled up from Machynlleth, thus piloting will be needed east of Talerddig. No. 9017 had a leading bogie, it was therefore an ideal choice for this type of long-distance piloting. This London-bound service avoided the usual reversal in Shrewsbury Station by running direct from Welshpool to Wolverhampton using the Coleham curve. In fact, it appears that both Nos 75020 and 9017 came off at Welshpool, used the turntable there, and then returned westwards. No. 75020 was seen again as pilot to No. 7818 on the down Cambrian Coast Express with twelve coaches (passing Talerddig at 3.30 p.m.), and No. 9017 came back with no load—this explains how No. 9017 ended up facing different directions in the two photographs. (*Dennis Bath's collection*)

Talerddig might have been famous among British railway enthusiasts as a nice place to watch trains, but it had a far more important worldwide claim to fame: it had what was, at the time of its building, the deepest rock cutting in the entire world. The original plan here (1858) was for a tunnel, but this was changed when the contractors found they needed a lot of stone to bridge deep ravines. There was some high-quality stone in the cutting, and the navvies also found a little gold. Work started on Talerddig Cutting in 1859 and it continued until September 1861. This is another photograph dating from Saturday 3 August 1963: blasting its way through the 120-foot-deep cutting is No. 7820 *Dinmore Manor*. The train concerned is the 10.20 a.m. Aberystwyth to Shrewsbury stopping service, and with only five coaches it needs no pilot locomotive. Visible in the right background is a 50-mph speed restriction sign, and this applied over reverse curves downhill for 2 miles. Further behind is the bridge carrying the minor road to Bont Dolgadfan. On my website and freely downloadable in the 'Sound Bites' section is a 1966 tape recording of the up evening mail train made from this bridge.

Below: At what has to be one of the more famous railway photographic locations, this is Bell's Bridge between Talerddig and Llanbrynmair, and a little below Talerddig Cutting. The date is Saturday 7 August 1965 and Nos 75014 and 75003 are hauling ten coaches up the steepest section of Talerddig Bank, 2 miles at 1 in 52, much of which corresponds with the 50-mph speed limit mentioned in the previous commentary. Although Alan Maund has clearly written the locomotive behind's number, No. 75003, on the original slide, this was a Worcester-based locomotive at the time. The railway here shares this narrow defile with the A489 (now A470) road and the fast-flowing Afon Iaen. For about 150 yards the railway is carried over the river by a 12-foot-wide 'big culvert', and just beyond is the 60-foot-high Bell's Bridge (Pont Bell). The extra width of the bridge is clearly visible for the double-track that never materialised. The original twenty pages of hand-written 'specification for works' bear silent testimony to the workmanship and quality of materials: this section required a more substantial permanent way than that between Moat Lane Junction and Talerddig. (*Alan Maund's collection*)

A little to the east of the site of Commins Coch Halt, the railway passes underneath the main road, as it climbs up to Talerddig. The road, river, and railway all make a 90-degree turn here, and this view is of the up evening mail train from Aberystwyth in the spring of 1966, just past the road bridge. The locomotive is a BR Class 4 4-6-0, and by this time they were the mainstay of all the remaining steam workings in Central Wales. There were eighty class members and all were built at Swindon, the last one, No. 75064, being the final exemplar of this popular wheel arrangement built in the country, but not the last numerically. But with new steam locomotives also being built in Britain, this looks very unlikely to be the case in the future. Despite its number being irresolvable, it is possible to work out which individual class member this is. Firstly, it clearly has a double chimney and twenty-four of the class were modified this way. Secondly, and more importantly, it does not have the BR2/2A inset tender, but instead the full width BR1B variety, the partition half-way along the top to limit coal capacity in plain sight. The BR1B tenders were used on the Southern Region allocated class members due to their higher water capacity, there being no water troughs on the SR. Only No. 75071 of the SR allocation was transferred to Wales (Croes Newydd, Wrexham in 1964), so this has to be the locomotive in this photograph.

Below: Another summer Saturday holidaymaker's train, and this time taken on 24 July 1965 between Cemmes Road and Commins Coch. No. 7820 *Dinmore Manor*, in typical 1965 condition and with no nameplate, looks to be working hard at lifting eight coaches up to Talerddig. The gradient here is 1 in 163, and it will be about another 4 miles before the punishing final 2-mile-long section of 1 in 52 begins. The first twenty *Manors* were built between January 1938 and February 1939, then there was a gap until No. 7820 appeared on 20 November 1950, and the final batch of ten had all entered stock by 29 December 1950. The Western Region of BR requested permission in 1953 for another ten *Manors* for duties on the Cambrian section, but unsurprisingly were allocated a batch of the BR Standard Class 4s instead. Twenty-two boilers were built for the first twenty *Manors* and eleven boilers for the final ten. Provision of spare boilers was routine, as it took longer to repair the boiler than it did the locomotive, and having a reconditioned boiler to hand cut down the amount of time spent out of traffic at the works. (*Alan Maund's collection*)

In the very early years there were thoughts of an agreement between the N&M and the GWR, with the GWR working the line. But at the N&M's half-yearly general meeting on 7 March 1863, the GWR's withdrawal was publicly announced 'with a feeling of deep regret'. The main reason cited was the incomplete nature of the permanent buildings. This is Cemmes Road as seen from a down train on 23 March 1959. In July 1863, and not long after its opening, a connecting horse-coach service to Mallwyd was advertised from here, and in those very early years there was even a refreshment room at Cemmes Road, too. The branch to Dinas Mawddwy closed in 1950 diverged here, but its platform was further to the right, behind the buildings and not visible in the photograph. The signal box was open from 4.10 a.m. until after clearance of the last train in the evening, but on Sundays it opened only for a short time in the morning and the evening. Cemmes Road Station lost its passenger facilities, as did many of the more rural stations along the line, on 14 June 1965.

Below: From Cemmes Road, an independently owned and worked branch line, the Mawddwy Railway, was built to Dinas Mawddwy and opened for both goods and passenger traffic on 1 October 1867. Initially there was a limited slate traffic from local quarries, which the CR worked forward to Aberdovey for shipment from the harbour. Traffic failed to develop and both the track and rolling stock were worn out by 1908, this bringing about its closure. A rescue plan was conceived and it was rebuilt to light railway standards, reopening in July 1911 and worked by the CR. It was eventually absorbed by the GWR in 1923, who then withdrew the passenger service in 1931, as they did with the Corris, Kerry, and Welshpool & Llanfair branches—all fallen victim to bus competition. Traffic declined further, and after flood damage in 1950 it closed totally. The first photograph is of Dinas Mawddwy Station in the summer of 1958; the station clock shows 5.30. Dinas Mawddwy was in Merionethshire, and that county still used steamrollers for the purpose they were intended for. FF4910 (a Merionethshire plate) is one of a batch of four ordered from John Fowler in 1937 to work for the County Council. It is seen between Towyn and Llwyngwril in 1964, and was still at work locally in 1969. It has survived into preservation.

Opposite: The railway tour of Central Wales undertaken by my father, Dennis Bath, and Eric Parker on 23 March 1959 started from Abermule at 9.20 a.m. behind No. 7827. There was a six-minute stop here at Machynlleth, and this is the view looking east just after 10.40 a.m. from the station footbridge. The service visible is the 9.55 a.m. Aberystwyth to Shrewsbury through-train, today hauled by Collett-2251-class 0-6-0 No. 2204. Ten years previously, this would likely have been hauled by a Dukedog, as seen earlier at Talerddig, but these were in decline by now and being replaced by the 2251s. To the left is the goods yard, and the signal box in the distance beyond No. 2204 is Machynlleth East, which had opened in July 1890. Prominent to the right is the 1863 goods shed: construction of this (and the engine shed) utilised the rubble-stone on site. Although markedly inferior for building purposes to the hard blocks quarried at Talerddig, it was an expedient choice at the time. But by 1949, the authorities were concerned over outward bowing of one of the main walls of the goods shed, and they became cracked and deformed. Just three years short of its centenary, it was replaced by a new goods shed (see the Introduction, page 8). Ironically, this was built during the period of goods traffic's greatest decline—and yet it has endured to this day.

Another view taken on 23 March 1959 at Machynlleth, but this time looking north and towards the goods yard in which the old Corris Railway station building was. The Corris Railway was built to transport slate from the valley of the Afon Dulas and its tributaries. The prosperous years for this narrow-gauge railway lasted until 1900, and dividends were paid until 1905. Nevertheless, the station building here dates from 1907, and there were also transhipment sidings to load the slate onto standard-gauge wagons. The Corris Railway closed for passengers on 1 January 1931, and the last freight train ran on 20 August 1948, after which there was flood damage which was never repaired. While both of the brake vans in the yard say 'Not In Common Use', that on the left also states 'Machynlleth RU No. 3'—'RU' stands for 'Restricted User', which indicates that it was confined to certain services. To their right is a Cordon wagon: these were used to transport gas to stations that did not have a mains gas supply and for platform and coach lighting. There were two varieties of Cordon wagons: one with two tanks along the length of the wagon (as pictured here and numbered W105), and one with nine short tanks stacked across the wagon.

Opposite: The view looking west on the same day as the previous photograph, the train on the right is bound for Shrewsbury with No. 2204, and that to the left is bound for Aberystwyth behind No. 7827. This site at Machynlleth was very restricted and confined by the Rock on the one side and the Dyfi flood-plain on the other. These natural constraints inhibited its development as the logical junction for coast trains to Pwllheli. The lack of bay platforms to handle arrivals and departures of the coast's passenger traffic was a major problem. The CR was well aware of this, and prepared a scheme that would partly address it before the First World War. Lack of space was also the main reason for abandoning the scheme to double the track ahead in the distance to Dovey Junction, and the CR had had ideas for this as long ago as 1871. Machynlleth West signal box is barely discernible, two finials of which are projecting above the far end of the station awning roof and just this side of the road bridge.

Below: The BR Standard Class 4 75xxx 4-6-0s that we have seen a number of times in this book had a tank engine equivalent, the 80xxx 2-6-4Ts, tank engines being regarded as more suited to shorter range duties. No. 80104 is standing in front of the coal plant at Machynlleth shed on Saturday 24 July 1965. This class only came to Central Wales because they were made redundant following the London, Tilbury, and Southend electrification. Twenty-one were reallocated from the Eastern Region to various Western Region divisions in July 1962. With the incorporation of the WR's Shrewsbury division into the London Midland Region after 1 January 1963, the allocation locally was: Shrewsbury (4); Croes Newydd, Wrexham (5); Machynlleth, and sub-shedded at Portmadoc (2); and Oswestry (4). Your author recalls seeing them on stopping trains on the former CR lines, and they did graduate at times to express workings. By April 1965, Machynlleth shed had an allocation of six, including No. 80104, but they were largely redundant by the time of this photograph due to a combination of dieselisation and closures. The official date of No. 80104's withdrawal, and in fact all of Machynlleth's remaining 80xxxs was the date of this photograph. Nevertheless, No. 80104 appears reasonably tidy, has shiny wheels, and its coal bunker is loaded to capacity. Interestingly, No. 80104 was another locomotive to end up at Barry scrap yard and yet survived to be rescued for restoration. (*Alan Maund's collection*)

Opposite: Close to the replacement goods shed mentioned earlier and with the locomotive depot partly visible ahead on the right is No. 75055. To the left is the goods yard, at a noticeably lower level. No. 75055 had been photographed on 24 July 1965; it had only arrived at Machynlleth shed the month before from Bletchley. There were now five of the class allocated to Machynlleth, and three of these were out-stationed at Pwllheli shed for fortnightly periods. Of these three, one was spare, one worked the freight service, and the third worked the Cambrian Coast Express on the coast section—the local coast passenger service having been turned over to DMUs earlier in the year. On summer Saturdays, all of Pwllheli's three locomotives were used on holidaymaker services. One of my lasting memories is of No. 75055 working the Pwllheli-bound portion of the Cambrian Coast Express, along the sea wall on the approach to Harlech, in the spring of 1966. Pwllheli shed closed on 5 September 1966, this marking the end of all steam-hauled passenger trains over the coastal section. (*Alan Maund's collection*)

Sadly, Alan Maund has not dated this photograph taken from a DMU at Dovey Junction. From the signals, it appears the service already at the station is bound for Aberystwyth, and that the one Alan was travelling on is heading for the coast line. Things could have been very different at Dovey Junction had the Dovey Reclamation Scheme, intended to be presented to Parliament during the 1861–62 session, gone ahead. This envisaged a substantial embankment nearly 6½ miles long that would contain the Afon Dyfi to within 3 or 4 furlongs of the Merionethshire bank. Vast tracts of estuary would have been reclaimed, in turn making a proposed bridge between Ynyslas and Penhelig much more viable. The railway would have been virtually straight and level in the vicinity of this photograph for nearly 6 miles. But representations from ship-building and fishing interests, plus concerns over costs, led to an application for a deviation in the 1862–63 session to bring the line south in the sweeping curve it follows here. Surprisingly, work did start on the direct line and the evidence can be seen nowadays by looking on Google Earth in the vicinity of Dovey Junction. (*Alan Maund's collection*)

Two more photographs taken of Dovey Junction, but this time the date is known—23 March 1959. The idea of a bridge near the mouth of the Afon Dyfi connecting Ynyslas to Aberdovey was pursued in the early 1860s before it was abandoned in 1865; one of these would have been a combined rail and road bridge. Instead, the line that exists today from Aberdovey to Dovey Junction ('Glandovey Junction' prior to 1904) was built for less than half the cost and in a fraction of the time needed for the bridge. But the resultant junction here was both very isolated and exposed: there is no settlement, no road access, plus it is especially vulnerable to flooding. The first view is looking towards Machynlleth from an Aberystwyth service, the old signal box prominent. Because of subsidence and decay, the old station buildings were replaced between 1957 and 1958, and the signal box in 1959 (its new replacement visible in the second photograph). An example of the operating inconvenience of Dovey Junction is the train at the coast line platform behind the new signal box. Visible is No. 2285, which has brought the train from Pwllheli but will now work light engine to Machynlleth. At the other end (and not visible) is No. 4575, which will take the train back to Barmouth, having worked light engine from Machynlleth to do so.

Two excellent but undated photographs of a DMU arriving at and then preparing to depart from Borth, in what appears to be ideal summer weather. This is an up eastbound service and heading towards Machynlleth, but somebody seems to have mixed up the destinations in the indicators above the centre cab windows. The indicator in the first photograph shows it is going to Aberystwyth (it is actually coming from Aberystwyth!), while at the rear, Wolverhampton (High Level) is displayed. The railway reached Borth from Machynlleth on 1 July 1863 and was extended to Aberystwyth on 23 June 1864; in the early days, there was even a through-coach to London Euston. Mention has already been made of the number of stations provided with refreshment rooms, and Borth was another so provisioned. The CR regarded them as good earners, and from the late 1880s most were leased out to a single firm. From 14 June 1965, Borth became the only passenger station between Dovey Junction and Aberystwyth, but its infrastructure seems to have remained remarkably intact—the water tank at the end of the down platform, the signalling, and a mass of telephone and telegraph lines. In 2011, the station building was opened as 'The Borth Station Museum' by a small band of volunteers who were loath to see it fall into disrepair. (*Alan Maund's collection*)

The initial use of *Manors* on the old CR main line was as a consequence of wartime air raids, when it became common to divert vital traffic to secondary routes. A daily munitions train was run in both directions from Llanelly to Chester via Aberystwyth, and the first *Manor* was noted on this in June 1942. The route first had to be upgraded to take Blue locomotives (17.6 tons max. axle load) instead of its previous Yellow category (16 tons max. axle load). The first allocation in the area was No. 7807 *Compton Manor* to Oswestry at the beginning of 1943. In the BR era they became synonymous with the Cambrian Section, and also worked the Carmarthen route from Aberystwyth. No. 7803 *Barcote Manor* came to Aberystwyth shed in April 1946 and stopped there for over eighteen years, until January 1965. We have seen earlier in this book, at Welshpool in early 1965 (page 57), the tip-top external condition Aberystwyth shed kept its *Manors* for working the Cambrian Coast Express. The same is true on 23 March 1959, to the great credit of the shed staff, as No. 7803 prepares to leave Aberystwyth. At this time and until 1961, a restaurant car was included and worked through to London. The regular weekday load was seven chocolate and cream coaches: three from Pwllheli, three from Aberystwyth, and the restaurant car sandwiched in between. The complete ensemble was well within the single-handed capability of one of Aberystwyth's *Manors*. The platform ticket is undated.

In addition to the CR main line, Aberystwyth was also a junction station for the route to Lampeter and Carmarthen. My father travelled down from Strata Florida to Aberystwyth on 9 July 1964 behind No. 7826 *Longworth Manor*, and arrived at 1.06 p.m. This is the empty stock being taken out of Platform 2 by No. 7806 *Cockington Manor*, squeezed in between some tank wagons and coaches. No. 7806, allocated to Wolverhampton Oxley at this time, will transfer the passenger coaches to the platform this photograph was taken from, Platform 1; then, at 5.40 p.m. No. 7826 will head back to Carmarthen. The engine shed at Carmarthen had closed a few months earlier, so No. 7826 will then have to go forward to Llanelly for servicing. Although through-trains between Aberystwyth and Carmarthen ceased in December 1964, the area around the former Platforms 1 and 2 is used today by the narrow-gauge Vale of Rheidol Railway, since this was re-routed here in 1968. The ticket is dated 23 March 1959.

2nd-SINGLE SINGLE-2nd

Aberystwyth to

Aberystwyth   Aberystwyth

Carmarthen   Carmarthen

CARMARTHEN

(W)   9/6   9/6   (W)

For conditions see over   conditions see over

9034   9034

It is a rather wet Thursday, 9 June 1966, and my father with Eric Parker made a return trip from Newtown to Aberystwyth. They went down on the Cambrian Coast Express, loaded to eight coaches, and came back on the evening mail train, made up of three vans and two coaches. In both directions they were hauled by No. 75016, which had recently paid a visit to Crewe works. It is in a livery of unlined-green used as an economy measure in steam's last years. The photograph is of No. 75016 standing in Aberystwyth Station, awaiting departure with the mail train. When built this class was turned out in a livery of mixed-traffic lined black, but from 1957 onwards, the WR alone decided their allocation should be in BR-lined Brunswick green livery. All the original WR allocation of twenty received this green livery, except two which had been transferred away from the WR before repainting. However, this locomotive is the one example that seems to have acquired green livery in error. In 1964, Eastleigh began overhauling WR and LMR examples, and re-applying green to those already carrying it. But black-liveried No. 75016, allocated to the LMR at Nuneaton, was repainted in lined green at Eastleigh in July 1964, and as stated above, was subsequently repainted in economy unlined green at Crewe during the spring of 1966.

This view again dates from 9 June 1966; it shows No. 75016 taking water by Aberystwyth shed that had closed in April 1965, although today the Vale of Rheidol Railway uses this building. No. 75016 will have to be turned before working back on the evening mail train, Aberystwyth having the benefit of a reversing triangle. The turntable that used to be here was transferred to Machynlleth during the autumn of 1939. One of the great benefits of the coming of the railways nationally was the dramatic improvements in postal arrangements, and it became a good earner for the railways. In 1807, Machynlleth was served by only three horse posts a week during the winter, but one horse post and two mail coaches in the summer. The financially stretched MWR got a welcome source of new income with the carriage of mail from 1 May 1865, and this carried on for nearly a century. On what became the CR, plans to use the railway began with a letter to the Postmaster General in March 1862. The initial mail service from Shrewsbury to Borth began on 1 January 1864, and a specialised Sorting Carriage was provided as of 1883. The last sorting carriages were used in September 1939, suspended for the duration of the war and then never restored. Mail trains continued to run until 1977, and at Aberystwyth a 'late fee box' was fixed to the station railings. Letters posted here required a surcharge, and were hand-stamped on the spot just before departure of the mail train, tonight behind No. 75016.

This photograph of the cliff railway at Aberystwyth is believed to have been taken in July 1965, and some of the details that follow come from a *Railway Magazine* article published the very same month. At that time it was owned by the Aberystwyth Pier Company Limited and was the only cliff railway ever built in Wales. Its construction was prompted by the building of the Lynton & Lynmouth, Bridgnorth, and Bristol cliff railways. The land was purchased in 1892 but construction did not begin until October 1895, and it finally opened on 1 August 1896. The article states the gauge is 4 foot 10 inches wide and 798 feet long, but these figures are in conflict with more recent data. Here at the half-way point the tracks diverge to allow the cars to pass one another. Initially the line worked on the hydraulic counter-balance system, but this was changed to electricity, for which double-haulage cables were employed. When water power was used the cars were fitted with tanks and an attendant's platform, but they have both been removed here. The sleepers were bedded on and anchored to the rock. (*Alan Maund's collection*)

Mention has already been made at Aberystwyth of the narrow-gauge Vale of Rheidol Railway, and that nowadays its passenger terminus is within part of the standard-gauge station complex. But it was not the case at the time of this July 1965 photograph, since prior to 1968 the railway had its own station adjacent to the standard-gauge one, which is visible in the background. Much of the line to Devil's Bridge follows the route of the proposed Manchester & Milford Railway mentioned earlier in this book. The very narrow gauge of 1 foot and 11½ inches was chosen because of the sinuous route involving curves as tight as a radius of 3 chains. The Act for the Vale of Rheidol Light Railway was obtained on 6 August 1897, it was to be twelve miles long and to start from Rotfawr Wharf in Aberystwyth Harbour. A goods service (mainly lead and timber for transhipment) started in August 1902, but regular passenger trains did not start until 22 December 1902. Absorption by the CR came on 1 August 1913, and they in turn became part of the GWR with the 1923 grouping. The GWR then pursued a policy of encouraging summer tourist traffic, and in 1925 built a 7-chain extension from the original narrow-gauge terminus to here by the main line station—where No. 8 *Llywelyn* stands in the sunshine—since 1948 under the ownership of BR. The ticket is dated 9 June 1960. (*Alan Maund's collection*)

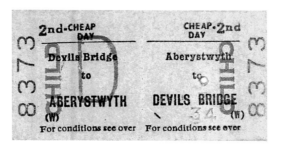

The black and white photograph is another dating from 23 March 1959, and is taken from an Aberystwyth to Carmarthen train as it crosses over the Vale of Rheidol tracks. To the left is the Afon Rheidol, and to the right is a stand belonging to Aberystwyth Town Football Club. The track being crossed over is the original route taken by trains to Devil's Bridge, and closed in 1968. Branching to the right is the track that led to the original station, situated off Greenfield Street that opened with the line and by this time the site of the Crosville bus garage. It was this line that was extended by the GWR in 1925 to the new station seen in the previous photograph. Straight ahead at the photograph's focal point is the engine shed, seen in close up in the colour view with No. 8 *Llywelyn* standing outside in July 1963. To the left of the engine shed are the remains of the Aberystwyth Harbour branch, formerly used for the export of lead from the quayside. This branch closed in 1924, although right of way was exercised up to 1930.

At 7¾ miles from Aberystwyth was the intermediate station of Aberffrwd, where there was a crossing loop plus watering facilities for the locomotives, consisting of two columns together with an elevated water tank. The up track of the crossing loop is rusty and was not in use at this time, thought to be July 1965, so this up train is replenishing its tanks at the 'wrong' water column on the down side of the loop. Note also that the signal posts have no signals on them. No. 8 *Llywelyn* is seen again, this is one of two locomotives built for the line by the GWR at Swindon works after the grouping, and part of their policy of encouraging tourist traffic. The Vale of Rheidol became Britain's only nationalised narrow-gauge passenger line, but in the early 1950s its future had hung precariously in the balance. 1955 seemed to be the year the pendulum started to swing in the line's favour. That year the Queen visited Aberystwyth, plus many high-ranking railway officials, and with the success of both the Festiniog and Talyllyn Railways locally, BR seemed to become aware of the asset it possessed. With the backing of Paddington, a vigorous local management, and widespread advertising, an unmistakeable sense of pride swept over the line—the locomotives were even painted in Brunswick green and given nameplates. In 1953 the total number of passengers carried was 14,105, but by 1956 it had almost doubled to 26,588. (*Alan Maund's collection*)

Below: The eastern terminus of the Vale of Rheidol line is here at Devil's Bridge, and in another view thought to date from July 1965, No. 8 *Llywelyn* has run round its train and will soon be heading back to Aberystwyth—a journey that can be repeated today. Devil's Bridge is a beautiful spot, 680 feet above sea level, and the village is famous for its triple bridge and waterfalls, but it could have had a very different railway history. A Manchester & Milford Railway scheme proposed a junction station at Devil's Bridge on its main line with a branch to Aberystwyth, but this came to nothing. When the narrow-gauge line arrived from Aberystwyth in 1902, it closely followed the original M&M route. By 1908, there were proposals for a continuation of the narrow-gauge beyond Devil's Bridge and over the hills to Rhayader and Llandrindod Wells—what a magnificent tourist railway that would have been, then and now! But back in the real world, after the demise of BR main line steam in 1968, the Vale of Rheidol line became BR's only steam operation, and this carried on until it was privatised in 1989. Today the line is owned by a charitable trust. (*Alan Maund's collection*)

The Manchester & Milford Railway has already been mentioned a number of times, and generally with paper schemes. Even one line that did make it to reality, the Llangurig branch, only had a single goods train ever travel over it. Yet in many ways one of the strangest things about the M&M was the railway it did actually build, open, and run a service on for many years—though it went to neither Manchester nor Milford, but from Aberystwyth to Pencader (Junction). The M&M was absorbed completely by the GWR in 1911, and with the track southwards from Pencader to Carmarthen already part of the GWR empire, it created a through-route of 56 miles and 29 chains between Aberystwyth and Carmarthen. Caradog Falls Halt was 11 miles and 68 chains south of Aberystwyth and was opened by the GWR in September 1932; it served the nearby hamlet of Tynygraig. This undated and unaccredited photograph shows the view looking north. Just to the south was the 86-yard-long Tynygraig Tunnel, seen in the second photograph as No. 7829 *Ramsbury Manor* pulls away from Caradog Falls Halt on 23 March 1959 with the midday Aberystwyth to Carmarthen service. Because of the difficult southbound 1 in 41 uphill start from this halt, any stopping service had its maximum load reduced by 20 tons.

This is the goods yard at the strangely named station of Strata Florida, seen on 23 March 1959 from an up service. Two men are busy with the hand-operated crane unloading a wagon, these sidings being taken out of use in April 1964. The name came from a nearby ruined abbey and the station served villages close by. The M&M north of Pencader (Junction) to Strata Florida opened in two sections; Pencader to Lampeter on 1 January 1866, and Lampeter to Strata Florida on 1 September 1866. It was from this area that the M&M was initially hoping to cross the hills to Llangurig via Devil's Bridge, but after a change of plan this route was abandoned in favour of a line via Cwmystwyth. The railway from Strata Florida to Aberystwyth was intended as a branch to be built after the mountain section. But with the difficulty of the mountain route and money running short, it was decided to build the line to Aberystwyth instead, which opened on 12 August 1867. The through-route from Carmarthen to Aberystwyth survived until the *Railway Observer* reported a proposed closure date to passengers of 9 September 1963, this later becoming 4 January 1965. It finally got moved to 22 February 1965, but the section from Strata Florida to Aberystwyth was closed earlier on 14 December 1964, due to flood damage not considered worth repairing given the imminent closure. The ticket is dated 11 June 1964.

Tregaron Station is pictured on Thursday 11 June 1964. In the down platform missing its smoke box number plate is No. 7814 *Fringford Manor*, complete with the 'wrong' type of tender for a *Manor*. Milk traffic was important for the railways in this area, and *Fringford Manor* had just dropped off six empty milk wagons for the dairy at Pont Llanio, the station before Tregaron. The engine history sheet for No. 7814 shows it had an unclassified repair at Llanelly shed between 27 April and 5 June 1964, and this was when it acquired the incorrect tender; the locomotive was also transferred from Llanelly to Gloucester in the June, so a busy month for *Fringford Manor*! The flooding that prematurely closed the line took place on 12 December 1964: a bridge sustained damage near Llanilar, and the track was badly flooded on this section. Although the records state the line was kept open to Strata Florida, the replacement bus service operated between Tregaron and Aberystwyth from Monday 14 December 1964 onwards, according to both the *Railway Observer* and the SLS house magazine. The answer to this conundrum, courtesy of John Livsey, Chairman of the Monmouthshire Railway Society, is that the bus service operated from where the up and down train services would have passed one another. The train crews operated from both Aberystwyth and Carmarthen, changed over where the three daily services each way crossed each other, and then worked home: one passed at Strata Florida, one at Tregaron, and one at Lampeter. The ticket is dated 9 July 1964.

2nd · SPECIAL CHEAP DAY	SPECIAL · 2nd CHEAP DAY
Tregaron to	Aberystwyth to
ABERYSTWYTH	**TREGARON**
(W)	(W)
For conditions see over	For conditions see over

2582   2582

Virtually midway between Aberystwyth and Carmarthen is the university town of Lampeter, it was the third largest town in Cardiganshire (after Aberystwyth and Cardigan). The station buildings and goods yard are both seen on 11 June 1964. The service arriving at the up platform bound for Carmarthen is hauled by a Hymek diesel, and in the goods yard is an English Electric Type 3 diesel, whereas steam is represented by a pannier tank in the down platform. The maximum speed allowed between Aberystwyth and Pencader Junction was 40 mph, and 35 mph onwards to Carmarthen. The signal box on the up platform was open in 1959 from 6.45 a.m. until the last train of the day had cleared; also, the box opened on Sundays for milk traffic from 1.00 p.m. until the return working from Pont Llanio had cleared. This route had a Blue GWR route availability, hence the use of lightweight *Manors*, rather than the Red and much more numerous but heavier Halls. The Hymek diesels were Red; however, a relaxation for this class allowed them on Blue routes subject to a 60-mph maximum speed, plus strict observance of all lower speed restrictions. The Hymeks could take 385 tons from Aberystwyth to Carmarthen, a *Manor* only 200 tons.

A latecomer to the railways of Central Wales was that from Lampeter to Aberayron, which had been mooted as far back as 1860. The Vale of Rheidol narrow-gauge line obtained powers in 1898 to build a 16½-mile-long railway south from Aberystwyth along the cliffs to Aberayron, but this ambitious scheme came to nothing. Also, prior to 1911 the GWR operated a road motor car between Lampeter and Aberayron, and a bus service to Aberayron from Aberystwyth complete with through booking from many GWR stations. But sentiment was strong locally for a standard-gauge railway of the area's own, and so, with finance from local residents and local authorities, the first sod of the Lampeter, Aberayron & New Quay Light Railway was cut on 20 October 1908. The line opened for goods on 10 April 1911 and for passengers on 12 May 1911. Under a 1909 agreement the GWR worked the line for £3,000 annually or 60 per cent of receipts, whichever was the greater. The connection with the main line was here at Aberayron Junction, and the Aberayron branch is seen curving away to the left in this photograph taken on 23 March 1959 from an Aberystwyth to Carmarthen service. This junction was 1 mile and 24 chains north of Lampeter, the signalling and pointwork controlled electronically from the signal box already seen at Lampeter Station. On the hill in the background is Twr y Deri (Derry Ormond Tower): this folly was built in the 1820s and is over 125 feet high, and at one time it was possible to climb the 365 internal steps to the top. It still stands today.

The author, his father, and Dennis Bath had the privilege of a return brake van trip over the Aberayron branch on Thursday 3 September 1964. These two photographs were taken on the return: firstly, at Felin Fach Station, and then the view looking back at the station and goods yard from the brake van on departure for Lampeter. I was lucky enough to be invited to travel in the cab of pannier tank No. 7437 over this steeply graded 1 in 42 uphill section, and can be seen (displaying my usual poor dress sense for a cab ride) in the white trousers by the signal box. Felin Fach Station once had a crossing loop, but this had been taken out of use by July 1963. The branch served an agricultural area and suffered from bus competition; 51,628 tickets were issued in 1923, but only 7,407 in 1949. The spur for withdrawal of the passenger service was the 1951 winter coal crisis, with the last passenger train running on Saturday 10 February 1951. Although announced as temporary it proved to be permanent, and officially so from 7 May 1951, despite local lobbying. Shortly after cessation of the passenger service, Green Grove Siding was opened about a mile from Felin Fach towards Aberayron. This served a dairy and transformed the fortunes of the branch.

The sole occasion the author visited Aberayron Station was on 3 September 1964, and in the first view, No. 7437 has arrived from Lampeter with the fireman bringing coal forward in the locomotive's bunker. The second is of No. 7437 shunting in the goods yard and visible are a number of coal wagons. When the line opened, the cost of conveying coal from Lampeter came down from 10s to 2s 4d per ton. As late as 1962, a dedicated parcels van was noted working over the branch and operating from Swansea. By this time it had ceased, but the still significant parcels traffic was carried in the brake van, having been loaded from the platform at Lampeter. There used to be an engine shed at Aberayron but it closed from 30 April 1962, the duties transferred to Carmarthen. Following the subsequent closure of Carmarthen shed in April 1964, the locomotive was supplied daily from Llanelly shed. The branch was in the GWR 'Uncoloured' category (maximum axle load of 14 tons) of route availability, so only the very lightest of locomotives were allowed. However, the 1959 working timetable shows that an exception was made with these 74xx 0-6-0s that were officially listed in the Yellow category (maximum axle load 16 tons).

There is steam escaping from various places below the running plate of No. 7437, and this is because of a steam pipe connected to its rear. There is also a hose pipe in the river below. No. 7437 is supplying a steam pump, which is filling the elevated water tank directly from the Afon Aeron; once full, the locomotive can then fill its own tanks. The most significant engineering structure on the whole railway was the substantial double-track river bridge that No. 7437 is standing on, yet the branch came to an end only yards after crossing over it in Aberayron Station. The reason for all this expense was the proposed extension to Aberayron Harbour, as the railway planned to continue on along the south side of the river beyond the station to enter the harbour on its south side. Strong opposition from the harbour company ensured that this never came to fruition. Another proposed line, and again never built, was included in the railway's title—The Lampeter, Aberayron & New Quay Light Railway. This was a 5-mile-long branch to New Quay via Oakford and Llanarth. Original rails made for the light railway (marked LA&NQ RLY) could still be found in the goods yard at Aberayron on 3 September 1964, the date of both photographs.

To conclude our visit to Aberayron on Thursday 3 September 1964, a final pair of photographs. Considering that this is a thinly populated pocket of Central Wales—in the 1950s, Aberayron had a population of only 1,270—the freight-only branch was surprisingly busy. Looking at the summer 1959 working timetable, when the engine shed at Aberayron was still open, there were three return journeys on weekdays and either one or two on Sundays (depending on the amount of milk traffic). The first service out of Aberayron was at 6.50 a.m., but previously time was allowed for shunting at Aberayron. The branch locomotive was then fully occupied with duties on the branch and shunting until 3.50 p.m., before taking the evening parcels and milk train to Lampeter at 5.25 p.m. and a final arrival back at Aberayron at 8.15 p.m. The maximum speed anywhere on the branch was 25 mph, with numerous restrictions to 10 mph. The level crossings were only protected with cattle guards preceded by warning notices 300-yards distant. The crew had to be prepared to stop dead before fouling any crossing—not easy with a heavy train on a 1 in 42 falling grade. Although Aberayron closed on 5 April 1965, the milk traffic from Green Grove Siding carried on diesel-hauled until 1 October 1973 (Pont Llanio closed in 1970).

GREAT WESTERN RAILWAY

WARNING IS GIVEN AGAINST THE DANGEROUS PRACTICE OF PROPPING UP THE DOORS OF MERCHANDISE TRUCKS FOR THE SUPPORT OF COAL WEIGHING MACHINES, FOR LOADING OR UNLOADING TRAFFIC, OR FOR ANY OTHER PURPOSE. THE GREAT WESTERN RAILWAY COMPANY GIVE NOTICE THAT SUCH PRACTICE IS PROHIBITED, AND ANY PERSON DISREGARDING THIS CAUTION WILL BE HELD RESPONSIBLE FOR INJURY OR DAMAGE THAT MAY RESULT.

FELIX J. C. POLE
GENERAL MANAGER.
MAR 1922.

GREAT WESTERN RAILWAY

NOTICE

STEAM ROLLERS, TRACTI ENGINES, MOTOR LORRI and similar Vehicles are stri prohibited from passing over plate of this Cart Weighbri

Any person disregarding th notice will be held responsible any damage which may resul

FELIX J.C. POLE.
GENERAL MANAG
Paddington Station LONDON.

Two more views taken on 23 March 1959 on the journey from Aberystwyth to Carmarthen behind the final *Manor*-class locomotive ever built, No. 7829 *Ramsbury Manor*. The first shows the branch to Llandyssul curving away to the left, the two lines coming together at Pencader Junction. The physical junction was 34 chains north of Pencader Station, the down platform and signal box of which are seen in the second photograph. The two lines were initially different gauges: standard-gauge for the M&M coming from Lampeter (1 January 1866), but Brunel's broad-gauge for the line to Llandyssul from Carmarthen (3 June 1864), the Carmarthen & Cardigan Railway. A Pencader Junction Station was built at the physical junction, but this was open only from 1866 to 1880. The problem of different gauges was solved by converting the line southwards from the physical junction to mixed-gauge in 1866, and M&M trains commenced working through to Carmarthen from 1 November 1866. However, the branch to Llandyssul was left as broad-gauge, converting to standard-gauge on 1 June 1872 and coinciding with the abolition of broad-gauge throughout South Wales. In fact, the C&C was the last to convert.

Another view of Pencader signal box, opened in about 1894, but this time taken on 3 September 1964. This was the date that my party had brake van permits for the Aberayron and Newcastle Emlyn freight-only branches. It is about 8.00 a.m. as the double-headed freight arrives from the Carmarthen direction, the locomotives working from Llanelly by now as Carmarthen shed had closed. It might appear that both are standard 57xx-class GWR pannier tanks—of which 863 were built and one of the most numerous classes ever manufactured in Britain—but this is not the case. The furthest locomotive is a 57xx class, No. 3671, but the nearest is from the 74xx class, No. 7437. Although visually somewhat similar, maximum axle load on the 57xxs was 16 tons 15 cwt, while the corresponding figure for the 74xxs was 15 tons 7 cwt. Weight restrictions on the Aberayron branch precluded the 57xxs, thus No. 3671 will work to Newcastle Emlyn while No. 7437 will run light to Lampeter for duties on the Aberayron branch. The second view is of No. 7814 *Fringford Manor* shunting in Pencader goods yard on 23 March 1959. Still running with the old BR symbol, it is perhaps relegated to secondary duties, as in a few days it will be stored awaiting overhaul at Swindon works.

On 11 June 1964, my father drove to Lampeter from Worcestershire, travelled on the midday train to Tregaron, then back southwards all the way to Carmarthen (behind a 'Hymek' diesel) before returning to Lampeter on the 5.50 p.m. It will be about 6.30 p.m. on a rather dull Thursday evening: the now-preserved No. 7827 *Lydham Manor* stands at Pencader Station while parcels traffic is dealt with. The signal box at the far end of the platform on the right closed in July 1967. The journey northwards to Lampeter, for which my father was fortunate enough to travel on the footplate the whole way, was almost entirely over former M&M tracks. This company had been leased by the GWR since 1 July 1906 and absorbed by them following an Act of 18 August 1911. An interesting throwback to the days of the M&M, even in 1964, were the mile posts. On many GWR routes the mileage shown was that to London Paddington, Pencader Station's figure being 260 miles and 27 chains. The same principle carried on all along the branch to Newcastle Emlyn, where that station's mileage was 270 miles 66½ chains. But not so towards Lampeter, where the station had a figure of 12 miles and 27 chains, as at Pencader Junction, the mile post mileage started again from zero.

The final visit to Pencader was on 3 September 1964, and after a misty start it turned out to be a lovely sunny and still day. Nos 7437 and 3671 arrived double-headed from Carmarthen, but by the time that this photograph was taken, No. 7437 had already departed for Lampeter light engine. No. 3671, a Llanelly-based locomotive, has already done some shunting in Pencader goods yard and is now taking on water at the down platform. While this was going on, the first up passenger service of the day from Aberystwyth arrived and departed. No. 3671 has charge of the Newcastle Emlyn branch freight and this will travel 34 chains north towards Lampeter before turning west onto the branch at Pencader Junction. The signal box at the junction had closed in 1929, and by now a member of the train crew worked a ground frame to gain entrance onto the branch, this including setting a trap point to protect the main line. Half a mile further on from the junction the crew will have to get off the train again, as there was an unmanned but gated level crossing to open and then shut.

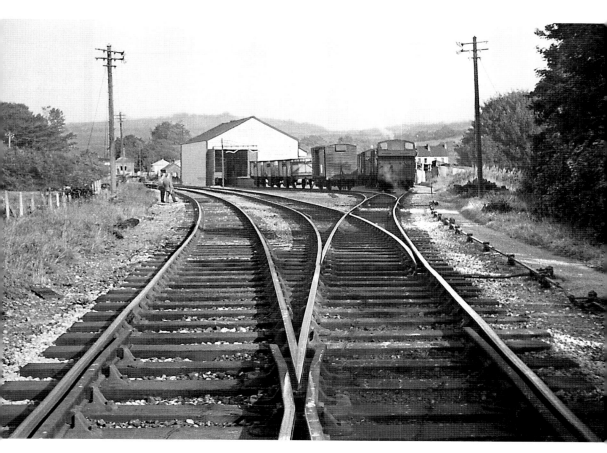

A prospectus was passed in 1853 for the Carmarthen & Cardigan Railway, the idea being to connect 'the important seaport and town of Cardigan' with London by a line from the South Wales Railway at Carmarthen. Cardigan was seen as serving the principle Irish ports and being several hours closer to London than Holyhead. Because of costs this was cut back to a line from Carmarthen to Newcastle Emlyn, with a view to it being extended onwards later; the Act was passed on 7 August 1854. The broad-gauge line was opened as far as Llandyssul (pictured here) on 3 June 1864, but with liabilities of around £1 million, this is where the works stopped. It was put in the hands of a Receiver in November 1864, and a horse-drawn coach gave onwards connection to Cardigan. Thoughts of extension westwards remained, but it was over a generation—thirty-one years—before this eventually happened. Llandyssul lost its passenger service from 15 September 1952, but even at the date of this photograph, 3 September 1964, there was plenty of activity in the goods yard (it was a market day), and I have a lasting recollection of the masses of parcels stacked up on the station platform. No. 3671 is seen shunting in Llandyssul goods yard, the station building being just visible around the corner to the left.

Our freight train hauled by pannier tank No. 3671 has now followed the valley of the Afon Teifi from Llandyssul and arrived at Henllan on 3 September 1964. The station had opened on 1 July 1895 but lost its passenger service from 15 September 1952. Total closure of Henllan Station followed in 1965, and although all the sidings look to have already been taken up, R. A. Cooke's track diagrams show that one siding remained at this time. Henllan Station had two curved platforms; the main station buildings were on the platform at which No. 3671 is standing, and these included the booking office, waiting rooms, and toilets. A smaller brick-built waiting room was provided on the other platform, and partly visible behind this was the signal box. In 1949 up to four trains daily passed at Henllan, but the box became superfluous after the demise of the passenger service and closed in November 1956, replaced by two ground frames instead. In December 1965, the loop, the remaining siding, and the ground frames were all taken out of use. Only the single track remained for trains to Newcastle Emlyn to pass along without calling, until the branch was closed in 1973; however, today, a narrow-gauge tourist line has been established at Henllan.

Below: Journey's end, as No. 3671 simmers away at Newcastle Emlyn having just arrived with the branch freight on 3 September 1964—this includes two petrol tanks for the fuel depot here. As already explained, the intention of the C&C was a through-route from Carmarthen to Cardigan, but the money ran out at Llandyssul. The 7-mile-long railway from Llandyssul to Newcastle Emlyn was opened by the GWR on 1 July 1895, and largely avoided major earthworks, except a 176-yard-long tunnel, by following the river valley. This railway never did make it to Cardigan, although at one time the GWR provided their own onwards bus service. There was just a single passenger platform, the derelict-looking track on the left connected to sidings, the goods shed, and cattle pens. The station itself was a long single-story brick building with five chimneys and a hipped slate roof. All the station's facilities were contained in this one building, including booking office, station offices, waiting rooms, and toilets (the 'gents' being visible in this view).

The broad-gauge Carmarthen & Cardigan Railway opened between Carmarthen and Conwil in September 1860, and it was extended through Llanpumpsaint to Pencader in March 1864. Llanpumpsaint, in the first photograph, is seen from an up train on a wet 11 June 1964 together with its modest wooden station building and signal box; the goods yard was behind the station building. Three miles and 11 chains from Llanpumpsaint was the next station towards Carmarthen, Conwil: the photograph here was taken on 23 March 1959 from an up service. Again, this is a modest wooden station, just behind which is the two-storey stationmaster's house and in front of which the signal box. Water was available for locomotives in both directions at Conwil, and it came from a small reservoir to the north of the station that supplied the tank in the distance. Note that the train the photograph is taken from has two milk tanks at its rear. Both stations had their goods facilities withdrawn on 2 December 1963, and both closed completely on 22 February 1965, although freight trains continued to pass through until 1973. Today, the Gwili Steam Railway has returned part of this route to working order, and has aspirations to extend the line to both Conwil and Llanpumpsaint.

Carmarthen, the southernmost destination in this book, and for hundreds of years the most populous borough anywhere in Wales. The first Carmarthen Station was on the South Wales Railway, but this by-passed the town and the station was poorly located for passengers, closing in 1926. The second station was opened by the railway we have just travelled along, the Carmarthen & Cardigan, in the distance, beyond both the road bridge and the single-track girder bridge over the River Towy. It had closed in 1902 when the station this photograph was taken at opened, after which the area by the C&C station continued as a goods depot; it is this third station that is still open today. This view is looking north on 23 March 1959, and nowadays the road bridge carries the A484 to Newcastle Emlyn and Cardigan. The locomotive on the left is No. 4134, locally-based at Carmarthen, and working a short parcels/mail train. The centre track it is travelling on was taken out of use in January 1972 prior to the station layout being revised. The numbers '3' and '9' that can be seen hanging from the passenger footbridge refer to stopping positions for different DMU car lengths.

It is 11 June 1964 and No. 7827 *Lydham Manor*, allocated to Machynlleth shed, is in the bay at the north end of Carmarthen Station ready to work the 5.50 p.m. to Aberystwyth. By this time there were only three passenger trains a day to Aberystwyth and the previous one was at 10.35 a.m., a gap of over seven hours. There were four return workings a day in the summer of 1959, plus an extra one on Saturdays. The striking building in the background is County Hall; completed in 1955, it was built on part of the Carmarthen Castle site replacing the Gaol. Steam on passenger workings was becoming something of a rarity at Carmarthen by June 1964; at the end of the 1963 summer timetable, the steam depots at Neyland, Whitland, Pembroke Dock, and Goodwick (Fishguard) were all closed. Carmarthen itself closed from 13 April 1964, its remaining locomotives and duties transferred to Llanelly. Of the three return workings to Aberystwyth in June 1964, one was covered by a Hymek (6.00 a.m. ex-Carmarthen and 11.55 a.m. ex-Aberystwyth), except on Saturdays, when it reverted to steam. Llanelly's allocation of *Manors* peaked at six in April 1964 when it gained those previously at Carmarthen, the last being transferred away in February 1965 and this coinciding with the total withdrawal of passenger services on the Aberystwyth line.

The choice of final photograph for 'The End' of this book seemed obvious, it having been made by the train crew of No. 1420 some fifty years previously. The branch to Presteign is curving northwards to the left, away from the Kington to Leominster line, and about a mile to the east of Titley Station. For this mile the two routes ran parallel but separate, and had done so since the opening of the Presteign branch: there was no physical junction where they diverged, except in the final few years. This was possibly the legacy from an earlier Act authorising a railway from Lyonshall to Presteign. No. 1420 is returning from having just worked the very last in-bound freight service to Presteign, and as various railway staff wanted to travel over the branch for one last time, two brake vans were included to accommodate everyone. While at Presteign the crew chalked the message in the photograph on the back of No. 1420's coal bunker, and in some ways it is pleasing to see how they have spelt the town. (The usual spelling of Presteign is with an 'e' at the end, but the railway officially spelt it without, 'Presteign', from its opening until April 1952, when the 'e' was formally added on. So the crew have used the correct railway version for 1964—your author can sympathise, spellings can be a minefield!) In the final years, the second parallel track from Titley Station was removed, and the physical junction was made at the point where the Presteign branch diverged to the left. The signal box at Titley seems to have closed in August 1958 and the junction had been moved a mile to the east by August 1959, the reality being that both were probably done around the same time. This is where No. 1420 is standing on Thursday 24 September 1964, the crew clipping the points on their way back from Presteign to Kington—this really was 'The End'.